AN EVOLUTION OF FAITH

AN EVOLUTION OF FAITH

How a Skeptic's Experiments
in Spiritual Paths Led to Faith in God

Hayley Wolfe

© 2024 by Hayley Wolfe

All rights reserved. No part of this book may be reproduced in any form without permission in writing from the publisher, except in the case of brief quotations embodied in critical articles or reviews.

Unless otherwise indicated, Scripture quotations are taken from the *ESV Bible (The Holy Bible, English Standard Version)*, Copyright ©2001 by Crossway, a publishing ministry of Good News Publishers. Used by permission. All rights reserved.

Published by Evidence Here Publishing

ISBN 979-8-218-38559-0 (Paperback)

Printed in the United States of America

This book is dedicated to the truth seekers.
The brave ones out there on a journey to know that truth,
no matter what it might be. I hope you are able to
learn something from my crazy adventures.

This book is also dedicated to my husband, Zachary Wolfe.
You always held my hand, no matter what part
of the journey I was in. I love you.

Contents

God Created Man ... Or Maybe Man Created God?
A Descent into Atheism   1

Stay Wild, Moon Child
A Descent into Wicca   25

It's Just Exercise, Right?
A Descent into Yoga   41

That Which You Think, You Attract
A Descent into "Self-Help"   53

Tat Tvam Asi – That Thou Art
A Descent into Hinduism   61

The Death of Self
A Descent into Meditation   69

And Then He Spoke
The Descending Ends   77

Evidence to Consider   89
Notes   97

God Created Man . . . Or Maybe Man Created God?

A Descent into Atheism

"Faith is the greatest cop-out, the great excuse to evade the need to think and evaluate evidence. Faith is belief in spite of, even perhaps because of, the lack of evidence."[1]

— RICHARD DAWKINS

I WAS BORN INTO a religious background, Christianity more specifically. I was raised in the farmlands of Southern Illinois. From Kindergarten through 12th grade, I attended Christian schools. My mom took me to church almost every week, and all of the friends I grew up with believed in God. I was shielded from a lot of the "outside world."

I listened to and traveled with my grandfather, whose mission was to carry the gospel to all the world through something he was inspired to start called Three Angels Broadcasting Network or 3ABN. Like most children, I focused more on myself and what I wanted to do. I would daydream about becoming something great to make my parents proud. Maybe, as the oldest of my parents' many children, I felt like I had to grow up fast and "be" something. This drive I developed would cause me to grow into quite an independent child/adult.

So, what caused me to forsake God? It was a slow process. I believe it started out with noticing how judgmental and hypocritical the words and actions of some of the Christian adults in my life were. Out of all of the reasons I have heard of people leaving a church they grew up in, those two are at the top, along with abuse, unfortunately.

I have long since forgiven everyone and can now see that many of the people I knew were doing their best in those situations and deserve mercy and compassion. I bring these things up because it is important for us Christians to be more aware of how our own words and actions might be affecting those around us. Children tend to see and hear more than we think they do.

The Bible says:

> *"Let no corrupting talk come out of your mouths, but only such as is good for building up, as fits the occasion, that it may give grace to those who hear."* (Ephesians 4:29)

This is not always easy, but it is something we should at least strive for.

There were also some things I was taught that I did not like. People would say, "You shouldn't investigate other ways of life. The paths that are not of God open doors to Satan's influence, and before you know it, you will be worshipping him." That is what was said, but my mind heard, "We are too afraid to learn about what other people believe, so stay in ignorance." I look back now and can't believe I actually ended up right where they told me I would, working with dark forces.

Unknown to my parents at the time, I felt heavy pressure to get baptized when I was 10 years old due to what some of the other adults in my life were saying. I went through the process of being baptized, but later that same day, some children my age were purposely teasing me and trying to upset me so that when I would get mad at their teasing, they could say, "You just got baptized, you have to be nice to us!"

After my baptism, my relationship with God had many highs and lows. I would go long periods of time not praying or having much to do with God, and when I felt God's call again, I would run back to Him with all my heart just to be met with a lot of resistance. Some of the adults in my life, Christian or otherwise, were the cause of a lot of that resistance. Sometimes, I would really be trying my best to follow God's ways, and a deeply religious adult would crush me by letting me know that they thought I was faking it. I questioned why I was even trying. Even as a child, I recognized how hypocritical and non-Christian their words and actions were.

As a child, I always took a heavy interest in foreign languages and decided to pick up Mandarin Chinese. I started to watch Chinese martial arts films to get more exposure to the language. Buddhist temples and Taoist statues caught my attention. These martial artists would be trained in the art of meditation and peace to become truly talented heroes. It captured my imagination as a child. I became curious about what these heroes were being taught. What secrets did they know? I found out that there really were monks and practitioners of these things in real life, and it was portrayed that they trained themselves out of mental issues such as anxiety and depression. These were things I felt plagued by at my age already.

My mom picked me up a Taoist book called *The Tao Te Ching* while we were at a bookstore. I told her it was just a classic philosophy book and that she had nothing to worry about. She trusted I would stay on the Christian path but didn't know I was looking for something different. I grew tired of the "Christian hypocrites" and began to wonder if the Christian path could really work.

I went to a Christian boarding school as a teenager in Tennessee. It took some time to adjust to things. I have a lot of fond memories of my time there. I'm so grateful I had the chance to go. I had a great experience! There, I met Christian adults who indeed showed the love of God. There were others, though, who were abusive and used God as a weapon. As a teenager, it's hard to know what to think when getting so many mixed messages.

I remember listening to a Christian radio station one afternoon. They discussed a conference where a Buddhist and a Christian could speak about their religions. The radio host was horrified at how, towards the end of the conference, much of the crowd converted to Buddhism. The Buddhist sounded so at peace and full of compassion, while the Christian had used scare tactics to get the crowd's attention.

After listening to this experience, I went deep into study. I learned about Daoism, the different kinds of Buddhism (especially Tibetan Buddhism), Satanism (the atheistic kind), Shinto, and many others—mostly Eastern philosophy. While I enjoyed the lessons that many fables of these religions taught, I still identified as Christian.

When I was in high school, a new popular book series came out that many of my friends started to get into. It was a vampire romance series called Twilight. That series did not interest me at all. I didn't like romance movies or books and still don't. I thought this series was really cheesy.

Some of my friends got into the series and started a coven. A coven is usually what you call a group of witches or vampires. They invited me to join, but I told them I wasn't interested. Later, the school staff learned about it and the students involved got in trouble. I got called into the principal's office and was questioned about what I knew. I told them I was approached about joining the coven but rejected the offer. They told me I would still get suspended because I learned about the situation and didn't say anything.

The next thing I knew, rumors spread like wildfire amongst the students that I had been a part of the coven and that I identified as a witch and vampire! I was horrified and got bullied because of it. Later on, when I began to look into witchcraft, this experience played into why I felt less reluctant to try it. People had already spread the rumor that I was involved long before I touched the stuff.

I was always in and out of communication with God during high school, but when I turned 18 and graduated, I became more interested in Him again. Unfortunately, once again, I received lots of pushback from people. Even some of the Christians I knew didn't like how seriously I was taking the Christian path. Due to this, I decided to focus on myself again rather than religion. I shut out communication with most people in my life, which was easy as a hurting introvert. I decided to use this time to figure out what I wanted to do.

I tried to go to college for Anthropology, but college was expensive, and I could only finish one year before I had to drop out. While I was in college, I started learning from my professors how the theory of evolution worked. I remember growing up, I listened to some pastors making fun of it by saying things like, "Yeah, for some reason, the world teaches we came from monkeys!"

Talking about evolution like that severely misrepresents the theory and made those Christians who said that seem very ignorant. I was one of the only Christian Anthropology majors in my university. Teachings on theories that I had never been taught accurately were confusing me, and I was having issues defending my belief in creationism. What my professors were teaching didn't sound so crazy after learning the details of what modern science teaches. It certainly didn't sound any crazier to me than God speaking everything into existence.

We can actually watch bacteria evolve under microscopes. They taught that single-celled organisms evolved into more complex ones as they adapted to the environment. These organisms would slowly evolve into the many living things in the world. Evolution is proven, as we can watch it happen under the microscope. Still, the theory of evolution (where we came from) and the Big Bang theory (how the process began) are just theories. They are no more provable than any other origin story people have come up with. It was to my detriment that I wasn't taught these views in the Christian educational system. It made us wonder what else Christians had misrepresented.

Many of the professors at the college compared the belief that Jesus was raised from the dead to the belief that Muhammad rode a flying horse into the sky. As they kept hashing on Christianity, I started wondering if I should do more research into how the Bible was made.

I was taught by these Atheist teachers that a council decided which books should be in the Bible and which ones shouldn't. People on internet forums would bring up points and questions like, "There was a book that wasn't added into the Bible just because it said the earth was round!" and "Parts of the Bible were added in later! We have proof.", and "Why should we believe that there were no human errors in the Bible? It is just a guess to say God would keep every piece of what those prophets wrote intact all this time." I had to sit with it for a while. I had never been taught to ask questions like these or consider information from history like the things they pointed out.

At this point, I had concluded that the New Testament's accuracy was more challenging to determine than the Old Testament's—at least from my understanding of it then. I have since learned that we have plenty of reasons to believe in the Bible's accuracy. You can learn much more from books on the topic than from the internet. Generally, if you "Google" these topics, you will get uneducated answers. I was too young at the time to understand that.

I encountered some responses from Jewish people on many of these topics. They were pretty good at defending the Old Testament's accuracy and had lots of archeological and historical proof to back up the stories. Some of them didn't even claim that all of it was totally true, which made it easier for me to believe. Books like Job were considered just a tale by some Jews, not real events.

As I looked more into things, I started to wonder, "What if the Jews were right?" I wasn't sure I believed they were right, but after a bit of time, the story of Jesus sounded too far-fetched. I let myself ponder what it would mean if none of it were true. What if God didn't exist? How would that change the way I saw life? I tried to imagine what it would be like if God didn't exist. I felt more doubt now than I ever had. I was so uncertain. So much new information bombarded me in such a short amount of time. I didn't want to believe in something that wasn't true.

One day, I was driving to my job and enjoying the beautiful weather as I pondered all the things I was learning. That's when it happened. It felt like my mind let go of something and then let something else in. Let me explain. I tried to see the beauty of nature as something that formed on its own, and then I saw it. I finally felt what it felt like to truly believe there was no God.

It was only for a few moments, though... you see, as I was struck and in awe of how amazing it was that all of nature came to be on its own, I thought of how amazing it was that something so complex came out so beautifully, but then I felt a familiar and peaceful presence and heard a whisper. "It is so beautiful and complex because it was created." I recognized God's presence. For a moment, I got to experience what it felt like to honestly not believe, and because of that experience, I was back to not being sure of what to think about who God could be if He was real and hoping it wasn't just my mind playing tricks on me. I knew what I felt but had become a considerable skeptic, triple-guessing my experiences.

Explorations of the Jewish Faith

I decided the story of Jesus was too difficult to believe in, but I wasn't ready to throw away the whole Bible. I decided to go to a Shabbat service at a synagogue by myself. I went to a Reform Jewish synagogue because I had heard they were more accepting of non-Jews attending their services. It was such a valuable experience. I went early to attend their Torah study class, which took place right before their Shabbat service. I was raised keeping the weekly Sabbath of the Bible that takes place Friday at sundown and continues till

Saturday at sundown, so it wasn't such a strange thing to go to services during these times.

They had a library in the synagogue from which you could borrow books, so I picked up a book on the daily prayers observant traditional Jews prayed. Many of these prayers are prayers written in the Old Testament and were quite beautiful. During the services at the synagogue, I got to experience their readings in Hebrew, the almost song-like ways they would read out loud from the Torah, and the sermons they preached, which were also very good. They sounded like many sermons I heard in Christian settings about King David, Moses, Ruth, etc.

I became friends with several of the Jewish people who went there regularly. They were very passionate about their heritage, loved to tell stories, and had friendly debates on many topics. Some of them were more traditional in belief, but some people, including the Rabbis from this synagogue, were not traditional. One Rabbi was a man, and the other was a woman. They believed that God used the Big Bang and evolution to create the world and that the 6 days of creation were most likely not literal days.

I appreciated what they believed because it fit better with what I learned in college and thus made the creation story more believable. I tried to investigate the creation topic more and found out that a lot more Jews and Christians were starting to preach this way about the creation story.

One thing I find important to this very day is that I got to celebrate each Jewish holiday while I was there. I had always heard of Passover because of the Bible's stories, but to experience it really put some things into perspective. Many of the "Sabbaths" you see in the Old Testament are what we now call the Jewish holidays. During Passover, they would tell the story of the Exodus out of Egypt and have food for us to eat to "remember" certain aspects.

There was another holiday on which people would sleep in tents or similar setups, and that also had to do with remembering things like the wandering in the desert that took place in Exodus. One holiday that stood out was a day of mourning. It was a day to fast and pray that the Messiah would return soon and that God would forgive your sins. Almost everyone wore black that day.

After having great experiences at this synagogue, I decided to try a more traditional one to see what it was like and how they differed. I tried a conservative synagogue and an Orthodox synagogue. I had heard these places were not as friendly with non-Jews, so to blend in a little better, I wore a head rap to cover my hair and dressed in a long skirt with a conservative blouse.

The conservative synagogue was very tiny. I didn't really talk to anyone while I was there. Unlike the Reform synagogue, both had their readings and prayers in Hebrew. I couldn't understand anything being said. I had learned how to read some Hebrew, but it wasn't enough to help me in these situations. I felt like the people sitting near me kept looking over, confused as to why I was having difficulty reading the Hebrew out loud with the rest of the room. The Rabbi would say something, and then the congregation would respond in Hebrew. I just moved my lips as if I was responding with them, feeling like I wasn't fooling anyone.

In the Orthodox synagogue, the men sit on one side, and the women sit on the other. No one really talked to or paid any attention to the women there, even after the service. Dinner was held in a different room, and everyone was invited to join in after the service.

I thought about leaving and not sticking around for it, but a couple of the older women approached me and tried to get me to stay and eat with them. As we walked through the halls, I saw beautiful stained-glass windows with Hebrew on them. I also saw a library. Unlike the Reform synagogue's library, which had books on every subject, this one seemed to only have Rabbinic writings like the Talmud, which are old debates on interpreting the books of law in the Bible. Christians might know these Rabbinic writers as the Pharisees, though some writings took place later than Jesus' time.

When we got to the dinner hall, they blessed the food, and we all lined up to serve ourselves. I wasn't familiar with any of the food there, so I got a few tiny scoops of a couple of things that looked like casseroles just to try them. I still have no idea what I ate, but whatever it was, it was really good! I just sat quietly while I ate, not wanting to give away that I wasn't Jewish, and decided to just listen to the men talk.

At the long table, an older man told many jokes and made his wife giggle. Some women were whispering about plans for certain Jewish holidays, but one young man spoke very loudly, which caught my attention. He was trying to debate what was written in the Talmud with some older men. I could tell he was very passionate about the writings of the Rabbis. He was talking about the "goyim," a word for non-Jews. He started talking about how when the Messiah comes, the goys would all come to the Jews to learn about God and begin serving God and his chosen people. He also said that, in the meantime, he wouldn't be talking to any non-Jews because he saw them all as very corrupt. I think he would have been upset to find out he was eating at the same table as a non-Jew…

Explorations of the Catholic Faith

There were many stressful and unfortunate things happening in my early 20s, and I wished for some escape. I thought about how nice it sounded to abandon my life and live in a pretty monastery as a nun. In my head, worshiping a God who may or may not be there, serving the community, and living a secluded life sounded more peaceful.

I decided to see if there were any traditional Roman Catholic cathedrals around where I lived. They always looked so pretty in the pictures. I found out there was a large one close enough. I looked up the times for mass (catholic services) and drove over one Sunday. It was hard to find parking; the place was massive and had many people. I was relieved that there were so many people because I figured no one would try to come up and talk to me.

I found a place to park and walked through a gate with a beautiful garden in it. There was a large statue of Mary and a place to kneel in front of it. I paused and stared at it, wondering what to expect from this place. I had never been to a mass before. I followed other people into the cathedral doors and saw many beautiful pictures hanging in the hallways.

When I walked into the sanctuary, I saw a fountain. Everyone was touching the water and then making the sign of the cross, which is touching the forehead, the heart, one shoulder, and then the other. I had always heard that particular action was a prayer that went… "In the name of the Father, the Son, and the Holy Spirit." I tried to mimic everyone around me to blend in. I touched the water, which was a thing called "holy water," and did the prayer. I didn't feel anything special after touching the water, but it did feel nice to say the prayer.

I looked up and around me. The ceiling went way up, and the walls were expertly painted with saints, angels, and Latin words. I knew a little Latin and could tell it was a prayer. There were statues of Mary and Jesus in several spots in the room. You could tell this sanctuary was made to leave a person in awe. I felt very comfortable there. It was the first time I had walked into a church in a couple of years, but it certainly wasn't like any church I had ever been in.

I saw people kneeling before taking a seat in the pews, so I did as I saw them do and then took a seat. I noticed a long bar at the bottom of each pew and wondered what it could be for. Some people near me pushed the bar down and knelt on it. I heard someone nearby call it a kneeling bench. I noticed many people kneel and pray while waiting for the service to start. I felt the urge to mimic them. That is the first time I remember asking God to reveal Himself to me if He was real.

Soon, I saw everyone stand up. This is when I noticed something very interesting. The service began to play out very similarly to the synagogues I had been attending. The priest would say things, and the congregation would answer back. He also read from the Bible in a singing manner, had a very short and to-the-point sermon, prayed scriptures, used incense, etc. I really enjoyed the service.

At one point during the service, everyone stood up and started lining up. They would take turns walking up to a priest to drink wine, called the Blood of Christ, out of a golden goblet. The line came back around to take what looked like a paper-thin cracker called the body of Christ. I recognized this as Communion, something that was done a few times a year in the church I grew up in, though in it, we were served grape juice and not wine. The Catholics here were calling this the Eucharist.

I got in line with everyone else, thinking to myself, "My germaphobe mom would be horrified if she saw that everyone was drinking from the same cup and that I was about to do the same thing."

As I came closer, I saw the line split weirdly, and I wasn't sure which way I was supposed to go. The priest beckoned me to him and asked me if this was my first time here. I said yes. He then asked me if I was a Catholic, to which I replied no. He proceeded to bless me and called to a woman nearby. She walked me away and explained to me that only Catholics could take part in the Eucharist and that if I was interested in becoming Catholic, they had classes for it. She also told me that the next time I come to mass, I can walk up with everyone else and cross my arms over my chest like an "X" to let the priest know that I am not Catholic, and he would bless me instead of handing me anything. I said thank you and went back to my seat, slightly embarrassed.

After the service ended, I decided to look around the large sanctuary. Many people were approaching statues, kneeling and praying in front of them. There were some areas where you could say a prayer, light a candle, and donate to the church. I was fascinated by everything I saw. I knelt before a statue of Jesus and prayed for belief since I genuinely did not have any belief in Jesus at this time. I figured if He was really the Son of God, He could work on answering my questions. I walked out of the church, stopped, and turned to face the massive building. I knew I would be back…

A little while later, I went onto the cathedral's website to see when the mass times were. They did them every day of the week, several times a day. I decided to go at noon on a weekday, hoping there would be fewer people. As I drove to the church, I wondered what I was doing. Was it dumb to be trying to enjoy something I had no belief in? There was no way Jesus was God, so this whole religion doesn't make sense. Why do I wish I could believe in it? Is it because I was raised going to church? This kind of church isn't anything like what I grew up in.

I pulled up to the church and walked in for mass. There were, as I had hoped, only a few people. The few people there were in the pews, kneeling on the kneeling benches and praying. It was so peaceful and quiet. The sun shone through the stained glass beautifully. I knelt to join silently in prayer. "God, if any of this is real, please show me. I have no belief in any of this, and I question if You exist. I want to believe; I just really don't."

When the service came to the Eucharist part, I approached the priest and made an "X" with my arms across my chest, as I had been instructed. The priest put his hand on my shoulder and prayed a beautiful blessing over me, and then I went back to my seat.

After the service, I went to look around again. I saw they were locking the doors and realized, unlike Sunday, they closed right after the mass. The priest who did the mass that day was a very young-looking man. Maybe around his late 20's to early 30's. He approached me and asked if he could help me with anything before closing. I apologized and told him I was new to all of this and had thought they were open all day. He welcomed me and offered to give me a tour of the church. That sounded fun, so I accepted.

He walked me through the entire church, showing me where they kept the crackers and wine, the choir room, where confessions took place, rooms for classes, etc. After explaining those places to me, we walked outside, and he locked up the place. He said he wanted to give me access to the building next door. It was a hangout building for the nearby Catholic college students. He gave me the passcode, and we walked in.

It had several couches and a big fireplace, all surrounded by bookshelves. I love books, so I got excited to see so many. He said I was allowed to borrow any of them. There was also a kitchen and outside sitting area that was fenced in. Upstairs were a few offices and a small room with 2 pews and a statue of Jesus. He told me that they put the extra crackers from the mass into the box beneath the statue of Jesus and that they believed that after it was blessed during the Eucharist, it had become the body of Christ.

When he told me that, I felt some of this place's magic lose its power. I just could not believe that to be true, and a part of me felt sad. Once again, I felt I could not fit into yet another belief system. I thanked him for taking the time to welcome me and show me around. I went back to my car and drove home.

Later, I decided to check out a different Cathedral in the area. It was an old one and one of the first Roman Catholic churches built in the area. It was very tall and pretty. I walked in for a mass and saw the priest I had met in the other church.

After the service, I went to say hi to him. I asked him if he worked for both churches, and he explained that this church is the main one he served in and that many priests from churches around the area take turns serving at that first church I walked into. He told me I was free to look around.

This church was much smaller than the other one but still beautiful and old. I saw a little drop box for money with writing on it that said, "For the poor." I thought that was very pleasant and put a little money in. I also saw they had free books on Catholicism. I picked up one and kept looking around.

Nearby was a confessional. I asked if I could get a closer look, and he showed me how it worked. He said it wouldn't be necessary for me to use since it is only for Catholic use. He also told me that if I wanted more information, we could meetup some time and he would answer all my questions. That sounded good to me, so we traded phone numbers, and I told him I would get back to him soon.

After a mass at the bigger cathedral I attended, I noticed a catholic bookstore within walking distance. I decided to check it out. The first things I saw when I walked in were a lot of saint statues and pretty rosaries.

A lady approached me and asked if she could help me find anything. I asked her what she would recommend for someone looking into Catholicism. She showed me a book called The Catechism. She explained that it held all the beliefs and reasonings of the church, including some things written by Popes. She also recommended trying out the rosary.

She gave me a little booklet with the rosary prayer and recommended times of day to pray it. As a person who did not believe in much, I decided it couldn't hurt to try it, right?

I bought the Catechism and a rosary and continued to look around. I liked the concept of the saints and how spiritual everything seemed, but it still seemed like I was just playing pretend. I thought, "If all of Christianity is pretend, Catholicism seems like the fun one."

I went back home to try the rosary prayer. Part of it involves asking Mary to "pray for us sinners." I liked the prayer, but I didn't believe in the Trinity, Mary hearing us, or any of it. Plus, the prayer was very long. There was a prayer for each bead on the necklace, and it was a long necklace.

Attending synagogue on Friday nights and Saturdays and then going to church on Sunday communicated to me that I was trying to fill something. Was it being raised believing in God and then abandoning the idea? Was my life just that stressful, and I was looking for an escape? Or was it what some call "the God-shaped hole in your heart" that He created so you would seek Him? I still wasn't very sure at this point.

I spend the next few months going to both the synagogue and the Roman Catholic church. I made friends in both and was invited to many events and people's houses. I even ran into one of the people I knew from the synagogue at the Catholic church during a mass! I wondered what he was doing there just as much as he wondered what I was doing there. It seemed we both were trying to find the truth, whatever that could be. I learned a lot from the Rabbis and became good friends with the young priest.

Unfortunately, I was being mentally and emotionally abused by a person during this time, and it got so bad that I saw my life as falling entirely apart. Schooling was too expensive, and I had gotten stuck in jobs I had never wanted to work. I never accomplished things I had meant to achieve, I had no real belief in anything, I was being abused at home, and nothing turned out how I pictured adulthood to be.

One winter night, I had to get away. I felt so hopeless. I decided to go to the Catholic college hangout building. It was late, so I figured I would be the only one there, and I was right.

I went upstairs and sat alone on one of the two pews and stared at the statue of Jesus. "What do I do?" I heard the door unlock down the stairs. The stairsteps creaked as someone walked up. "Hayley, is that you?" I turned to see my priest friend. I said, "Oh hi! Just wanted some time to think and thought a quiet place like this was a good spot." "No better place than in Jesus's presence for that." he said, smiling. "Are you doing ok? I'm here if you need someone to listen."

It was hard for me to keep the tears in. He could see that and sat down next to me. I told him I was having a tough time lately. I only went into a little detail. He was very kind and told me he would pray for me. He told me I would make it through because God would be my strength. I thanked him and told him I should go, it was getting late...

Explorations of the Buddhist Faith

I eventually stopped going to the synagogue and the Catholic church. I appreciated what I had learned and the people I had met, but I had reached the point where I just couldn't believe any of the stories anymore. I tried to find other ways to inner peace.

I heard that eating healthier, doing more relaxing exercises such as yoga, and learning meditation could all help a lot. I started to be more aware of where my food was coming from. Eating better was helping me to think more clearly.

One day, I looked up a beginner's yoga video on YouTube to try it. In my living room, I sat in front of my laptop and listened. The yoga instructor started with breathing exercises. I didn't know we needed things like breathing exercises, but she explained how they could help with anxiety management and bringing yourself "more into your body." I didn't understand what she meant, but I followed along.

After that, she taught some basic yoga poses and explained that you weren't just "doing poses" but "flowing" between them in smooth transitions. That is why many yoga classes call their classes "Yoga Flow."

She ended it with a pose called Savasana, which she explained meant Corpse Pose. In it, you are on the ground, lying on your back. You are trying to relax every muscle and completely quiet your mind. Just focus on your breathing. I didn't know then, but this was the beginning of learning a form of meditation. After the session, I felt a bit more relaxed. I decided that day to try and follow along with a yoga YouTube video at least a couple days a week.

I had a very loud and overactive mind. I was never at rest. I didn't know until later in life that I had an anxiety disorder. It was no wonder I found an interest in meditation. I heard that many Buddhist monks had learned to calm their minds by using it.

I decided that maybe religion wasn't for me, but philosophy, on the other hand, I was very open to exploring. From what I understood, you could separate Buddhist philosophy from the Buddhist religion and apply it to your life.

I tried reading some books on Buddhism and quickly found myself disagreeing with many of them. They taught me that life is just suffering, which, in my experience, doesn't have to be, so I disagreed quickly.

Another thing I disagreed with was reincarnation. I had been led to believe that Buddhism was just a philosophy that did not require faith, but it takes a lot of faith to believe in something like reincarnation. Rather than discount the entire religion over my disagreements, I thought I could still learn something about stilling my mind.

I decided to try going to a Buddhist temple to see if I could learn anything from them. I looked online to get the address of the nearest one and found one only 20 minutes away. I found a list of group meditation times on their website, picked one, and headed over the next day.

When I pulled up to the temple, I was very confused. It appeared to me to be a small, remodeled house. I wasn't sure I had come to the right place, but then I saw other people pulling up in their cars. I later found out that most of the Buddhist temples near where I was living were all houses that had been turned into temples. They were all Vietnamese or Tibetan temples.

As people started exiting their cars and walking in, I followed. When I entered the door, I saw the area we would be meditating in on my left and a small shop in a room straight ahead. I was very interested in seeing what a Buddhist temple would sell, but I turned to the left and followed everyone into a larger room that looked like it used to be a living room.

The room was completely empty except for maybe 12 sitting pillows on the floor, a box containing books, and a very long table covered in various large gold Buddha statues and what looked like decorations. Upon further investigation of the long table, I realized I wasn't looking at decorations. I was looking at offerings. Small bowls of water, fresh fruit, flowers, and coins were all over it. Besides the three giant Buddha statues, there were also many small gold ones. They were different incarnations of the Buddha. The whole setup was stunning.

As a few people came in to offer fresh flowers and fruit to the statues, a man wearing Buddhist monk robes came in and sat on the pillow facing everyone. I saw people grabbing books from the box at the entrance to the room, and I picked one up.

I took a seat on one of the pillows and opened the book. It had a Tibetan script on one side and the English meaning beneath it, but I didn't see any Romanization of the Tibetan script, so I wasn't sure how to pronounce the words.

As soon as everyone took a seat, the monk asked us to turn to page 4 and speak the prayers together. I turned to that page, and everyone started saying words in this foreign language. I couldn't read any of it, so I tried to mimic what I heard. I looked over at the English meanings of what we were praying.

We went over several prayers to Buddha and then to the previous teachers of the temple, the ones who had already passed away. All of these prayers asked that the Buddha and these dead teachers help guide us to enlightenment so we can finally escape the wheel of reincarnation.

As we prayed these prayers, I felt even more confused. I had heard people say that you didn't have to have faith in things to be a Buddhist. This didn't seem like a philosophy to me. I could now see and understand the reason Buddhism is called a religion.

After we finished the prayers, the monk told us we would be in silent meditation for 30 minutes. He told us that if our minds wandered at all, we should bring our focus to our breathing. And so, we began.

I was not able to turn my mind off. I kept bringing my thoughts back to my breathing, but then I was just thinking about how my breathing sounded, and I thought about all the sounds I was hearing in the room. As always, words were still forming in my thoughts. I couldn't figure out how to obtain complete silence like we were being encouraged to do.

After what seemed like forever, I noticed myself opening my eyes and looking to see if a clock was on the wall. "Wasn't this only supposed to be 30 minutes?" I decided to keep trying to fight my thoughts to find the silence. Finally, the monk started gently hitting a sound bowl. It sounded so beautiful. "Wow, that felt like 2 hours, but it really had been only 30 minutes." He ended our session by wishing blessings upon us, and then we all got up and left the room.

I wanted to see what this temple store sold, so I went straight there. It was small, but it had a collection of books. There were books on Tibetan Buddhism, meditation tips, collections of prayers, and books by the Dalai Lama. They sold prayer wheels, which you pray while spinning to send the energy of the prayer out to the world. They were very colorful.

I also saw long beaded necklaces with mantra books. They reminded me a lot of the Catholic Rosary. Just like the rosaries, you had something to meditate on or say per bead on the necklace. In the case of the Buddhist beads, though, your goal was to get better at meditation as you used them. After looking around for a bit, I decided it was time to leave.

Later, I went to an outlet store and bought a Buddha figure and some incense. When I got home, I set the Buddha on a stand outside and burned incense in front of it. I thought about trying my luck with Buddha and wondered if he was capable of answering prayer like I had heard he was. I asked him to help me find peace and silence of mind, and then I sat in front of the statue to practice meditating. I listened to the birds chirping and took in the smell of incense.

I focused on my breath, and then...there it was! For about 5 seconds, no words were forming in my head! I was very excited because those 5 seconds were the most peace I had felt in a long time. I wanted more.

I practiced meditation in this way several times a week. The longest I could find the peaceful silence was about 7 seconds, but it made a world of difference in how I felt.

For those of you who don't experience an overactive mind, this may not seem like much, but for someone like me, it gave me hope that I could find peace.

One day, just out of curiosity, I decided to drop by a Hindu temple. I didn't know anything about Hindus, only that they had many gods and that Buddhism came out of Hinduism. The temple I went to was huge. It was so beautiful! Unsure of how to approach such a building, I waited for a few people to walk in so I could follow where they went.

When I first came in, I was met with a very warm welcome. They asked if it was my first time there, and I said yes. They pointed me to a room where you were to take off your shoes and leave them in a cubby. After I did that, they pointed up a staircase and explained to me that the temple was up there, and no one could enter wearing shoes.

When I reached the last step, I saw a large room with many large altars and statues of gods and goddesses. Seeing that I looked a bit lost, a man approached me and asked me if he could show me around. He mentioned that he was very passionate about Hinduism and would love to teach me a little about it.

I accepted, and he walked me around the room. He took me to each altar and explained a little about what each of these gods could do for a person. I noticed many fresh flowers and fruits offered on these altars. Many devotees were in the room, bowing to the god of their choice as we walked around.

Finally, we came to the last god. He had the biggest altar in the room, and his statue was huge. It was explained to me that his name was Ganesha, an elephant-looking god. He was known as the remover of obstacles and was the god this temple was named after. I was very impressed by this "remover of obstacles," but Hinduism seemed like a very farfetched religion to me.

After the tour was finished, I thanked the kind man and went home.

Explorations of the Satanic Faith

I had found some of the silence I sought in Buddhist meditative practices, but I wasn't so sure it was because of Buddha. At this point in my life, I could no longer believe in anything spiritual.

A thought came to mind... "God won't reveal Himself to me in a way that I am sure He is real, but surely if Satan and his demons are real, they would show themselves. If they appeared, then I would know that God is real." I was pretty sure at this point that Satan was just another myth and that there were no such things as demons.

I wasn't sure where to start, so I tried looking up Satanism. I found out that the majority of Satanists were Atheists. Strangely, so many of the Christians I knew had told me that Satanists worship Satan. This was just another thing I found that made me think Christians were very ignorant.

I looked up what Satanists believed and learned about a man named Anton LeVay, the founder of the Church of Satan. He did not believe in the story of the Bible but liked what Satan represented. In his eyes, Satan represented freedom from the oppression of a selfish God ("LaVeyan Satanism").

In this "church," anything that pleases you is allowed unless it hurts someone else. That idea didn't sound so bad to me. Why not enjoy life how you want and still be able to say you are a good person since you aren't hurting anyone?

I found all this interesting, but this is not the kind of Satanism I was looking for. The other kind of Satanism I learned about was the religious kind. These are people who do actually worship Satan, usually in the form of Baphomet. I wanted to understand how it is that they work with demons. In my head, summoning a demon was worth the risk. I figured that after I had proof of the spiritual realm by doing that, I could then go to God and believe in His story.

I learned about Alchemy and a thing called The Seal of Solomon. Supposedly, King Solomon had a seal or ring that gave him power over demons and other supernatural things.

The seal was the Star of David, and various designs were around it. A later form had alchemical symbols around it. Jewish historian Josephus talked about the seal as far back as Jesus's time. Judeo-Christian mystical texts like the Testament of Solomon also refer to it.

I then learned about the Key of Solomon, in which King Solomon supposedly wrote down the sigils necessary to summon different kinds of demons for the purpose of experimentation.

A sigil is a type of symbol used in magic. It is a pictorial signature of a deity or spirit. I learned that to summon a demon, you must write down its sigil and chant its name. Supposedly, it would give you what you wanted in trade for something, usually serving the demon or promoting it to other people ("Seal of Solomon").

I found information online from people who claimed they had experience with these things or had studied them extensively. They said that some demons are friendlier than others, so you needed to be careful about who you tried to summon.

I was slightly nervous. On the off chance that this really worked, I didn't want to have to serve or work with a demon. I was trying to see if there was really anything out there. I tried to look up the sigils of different demons. There were very accessible collections of these symbols and information on these demons collected by the Catholic church over time, primarily by exorcists.

I found a list of "friendlier" demons and chose one known for sharing the hidden knowledge of the universe. I will not be writing his name here. I learned everything I could about him for "safety reasons." I chuckle at that now because if I had really been worried about safety, I probably shouldn't have been trying to find a way to talk to a demon.

I prepared everything. I wrote down the demon's sigil and followed the steps I had learned from others. I waited. It was dark and quiet. I waited and waited. After no luck, I tried again the next day.

The waiting felt long, and I was starting to feel dumb for even thinking anything would happen. I became more aggressive with the process, pushing the limits. This was the spirit realm's last chance to let me know it was there. But nothing...nothing happened.

It was there, alone and in the silence, I came to the conclusion that man had created God.

Stay Wild, Moon Child

A Descent into Wicca

> "Once you realize that the universe is made up of processes, not things, you are really on a roll, for what makes life truly interesting are the connections between events."[1]
>
> SILVER RAVENWOLF

NOW THAT I was convinced that God was a made-up concept, I decided to study the Theory of Evolution and the Big Bang Theory in more depth. After all, these are the things taught in most schools, right? I realized that these, like religion, require a certain amount of faith. The more you look into most kinds of science, the more you see how much we don't know and how much guesswork there is.

I didn't mind putting my faith in the scientists. If the theories they came up with were the best we had, well, then that was the best we had. I was willing to accept how much we couldn't understand.

I started reading books like *The History of God* by Karen Armstrong and *The God Delusion* by Richard Dawkins. I listened to some of

Richard Dawkins's debates and speeches and soon stumbled across Christopher Hitchens, another well-known spokesman for Atheism.

All of these sources told me the same thing: God is a creation of the human mind. Early humans had no way of understanding the world around them. They had no way to understand the purpose of the sun and moon, no way to understand what happened after they died, no way to establish better order among the people, no way to explain what dreams were, and so on.

Ultimately, gods, mythology, and magic were our best attempts at understanding life and how to function. But now, they would go on to imply we have science! We can see microscopic things and explore deep into space. Maybe God lived on the highest mountain on Earth? We climbed that mountain and didn't see Him. Maybe God lived in the clouds? We flew our planes up there and didn't see Him. Perhaps He is just past the edge of our stratosphere. We sent rockets into space and didn't see Him. Maybe He is in deeper space? Sounded to me like maybe He was never there to begin with.

At this point, I became quite comfortable calling myself an Atheist. I went to a pastor I liked to give him a chance to defend his position. His answers to my questions weren't solid enough for me; they required too much faith.

> *"And even if our gospel is veiled, it is veiled to those who are perishing. In their case the god of this world has blinded the minds of the unbelievers, to keep them from seeing the light of the gospel of the glory of Christ, who is the image of God."* (2 Corinthians 4:3-4)

The "god of this world" that this verse is referring to is Satan. These verses answer why a person might not be able to see or believe, but believing it also requires faith, so I saw this as no answer at all.

At this point, life got worse and worse for me. It got so bad that I decided to move away from everyone and everything to California, where I had some family. I had to start all over again, and the first thing I did was decide to think about what I wanted to be in life.

While trying to figure out schooling and career stuff, I enjoyed dating my now husband, Zack. We didn't talk a lot about religion with each other because I wasn't very respectful of Christianity, and he didn't want to come off as "preachy" while talking to me. He was always so sweet and encouraging of me in all my endeavors. We were very in love.

I remember one night, while we were talking, I told him I would do anything for him. He said, "If you want to do something for me, just pray." I didn't believe in prayer, but I told him I would try to do it every day. This ended up being a lifeline for me later. I didn't always do it each day, but my prayers were almost always the same, "Please bless Zack." I didn't pray for myself because I didn't think it would do anything.

I don't remember exactly what brought this question up in my mind, maybe something I saw or heard about, but I wanted to know why there were people out there calling themselves witches. I didn't believe in spiritual or unseen forces, so I couldn't imagine why anyone would believe in something like magic…which I found out wasn't even the correct spelling for the "real" kind. That was spelled "magick."

If spells really worked, don't you think everyone would know about it? I searched online to see what people said. Some people agreed with my idea that everyone would be doing it and that we would have video evidence if it was real. Other people told stories about how they cast spells, and they would work, or something weird would happen.

I concluded that I wouldn't learn anything from reading what people said about it online, so I decided that there was only one way to find out for myself.

I love books. I could read all day. I went to the local library, wondering if I could find any books on the topic, and to my surprise, there was an entire section for witchcraft and the occult. I spend many hours in the library, several times a week, reviewing these books. I learned that magick was not like what we would see in stories like Harry Potter. Instead, it was about manipulating "energies."

The way it was described sounded similar to things we understand about science. On a microscopic scale, we know that everything in the universe is made up of the same stuff. You and I, a flower, the planet Saturn, every material thing you can think of, is made of the same baryonic matter. Atoms are composed of protons and neutrons, which are, in turn, composed of quarks and electrons, etc.

We also know about the Law of Conservation of Energy and Mass, which states that mass cannot be created or destroyed. That means that when something appears to be destroyed entirely, it isn't. That also means that if something appears before you seemingly out of thin air, it didn't. The building blocks for it were there all along on a microscopic scale.

These books pointed out that energy is what it takes to change matter and that magick is just a manipulation of energy. Since I understood the "science" behind it, I was curious to see if a person could, in fact, manipulate energy like this.

If I was going to test this stuff out, I would need to follow all of the instructions. I started a "Book of Shadows," which is like a witch's journal. I wrote down all the essential information I would need for casting spells, such as information about the moon phases and crystal usage.

If you have never been involved in these things, crystal work and Astrology may sound like silly beliefs. I know I thought they sounded silly. I hadn't realized there were explanations for all of these things, though.

The Argument of Crystal Work

There was an experiment done by Masaru Emoto involving water crystals. Here is a quote from *The Times Square Chronicles* that explains it well...

> *"In his book, Dr. Emoto used Magnetic Resonance Analysis technology and high-speed photographs to prove how water reacts to words and music. If water heard positive, loving and kind words*

the result was beautiful crystals. If the water was exposed to fearful, hate and unpleasant words the water turned dark and ominous. His research also showed us how polluted and toxic water, when exposed to prayer and intention can be altered and restored to clean, healthy water..... His work brought in the question, if water is affected by the words, intentions, and energies, what about human beings, who are made of 60% water? If we transform the water and thoughts we are made of, what else is possible?"[2]

The website also shows pictures from the experiment. The argument about crystals touching or being near you is similar. In the New Age, you hear talk of how crystals vibrate differently depending on which crystal they are (as all atoms vibrate at a microscopic level) and that these vibrations being near us affect our body and mind. There are also patterns across thousands of years in many cultures, classifying crystals for similar uses.

For example, amethyst was believed to promote relaxation in the body and mind in many parts of the world. I wondered how all of these things could be coincidences. Was there something to this talk of vibrations and energy? These examples and many others not listed here are some of the reasons I started believing in these things.

For anyone starting to ponder these things due to the information I have provided, I would like to state that the experiments with the water crystals have since been debunked (Novella). I wanted to show New Agers that I understand where they are coming from and Christians that people don't believe in these things without being given reasons. Sometimes, we later discover that these "reasons" were not as solid as we once thought.

The Argument of Astrology

When reading these witchcraft books, they repeatedly mentioned how important it is to know your star and moon signs. Most people who don't understand astrology very well have at least heard of sun signs. Depending on when you were born, you may fall under the sign of Aquarius, Taurus, or a number of others. Falling under a certain sign was supposed to say something about your personality.

I always had a hard time believing that. I was born on the first day of Aries. When you read the characteristics of an Aries, it sounds nothing like me. Many people have felt that their sign doesn't "match" them. Some people say the one they fell under matched them entirely. When I read Zack's sign information, it described him perfectly. I wondered how that could be a coincidence. I thought, "Maybe it is a coincidence since my sign doesn't describe me."

I like to give people a chance to explain their points of view, so I did some asking and searching. I was told that a sun sign is basic and only holds some of your information. You also have a moon sign, which says more about your inner being. If you knew what time you were born, you could also get more accurate information about where all the planets were when you were born and how that says even more about you.

After this, I bought a thick book on Astrology and learned everything I could about the topic. The main reason Aries didn't seem to describe me well, I discovered, was that I was just barely born an Aries. I was on the edge of Pisces. Pisces didn't describe me perfectly, but it described me better than Aries. I was told I was a bit more complicated because of when I was born and that I shared traits with both sides.

After researching this topic in more detail, I concluded that there was something to this whole thing; maybe we just didn't understand it very well yet.

I learned that the moon's current phase was also supposed to influence your mood and success. Certain spells were supposed to work better during different phases.

One thing I remember reading about in these witchcraft books was a question about gravity. If the moon's gravity pulls the tides of the ocean, then don't you think it can affect your blood? How would that affect your thoughts and mood during a full moon? What a curious question. Both are liquid, right? Here is a quote from an article on healthline.com.

> *"The idea that a full moon can stir up emotions, provoke bizarre behavior, and even cause physical illness isn't just a literary trope. It's a strongly held belief, even today. In fact, one study says that nearly 81% of mental health professionals believe the full moon can make people ill."*[3]

That is a considerable number of mental health professionals. I even heard about statistics showing hospitals filling up during full moons. If the moon can have such an effect on us, could other planets also affect us?

I did not fully understand how these things could work, but after studying astrology in depth, seeing how well it predicted lots of things, and reading what all these books and people were saying about the moon, I decided that it was all very possible. They made it sound very scientific and factual.

That being said, let's talk about what we actually know. What's up with ER visits increasing during the full moon? Well, here is what just one of many articles says about it. This is from *yourworldhealthcare.com*...

> *"In his published study for the lunar effect on hospital admission rates or birth rates, Professor Jean-Luc Margot (UCLA dept. of Physics and Astronomy) delves into the myth behind healthcare and the moon. After assessing a wide range of reports and studies on the moon and how it links to hospital admissions, birth rates and complications, and behavioral disorders, Margot did not find a direct correlation and stated: "We can say with certainty that none of these areas of human affairs are affected by the moon.""*[4]

When I was exploring these things years ago, I decided there was enough out there to prove a case for astrology, but looking back on it, I really should have researched why science disagrees with astrology. If you are someone who still believes in these things, I would highly encourage you to look into the arguments against it. I think it is always wise to be educated on both sides of any argument so we can draw better conclusions.

Let the Experiments Begin

I don't remember every experiment I tried, as I no longer have my Book of Shadows, but I would like to write down the results of some of them here. When I studied witchcraft, I found that I liked the practices in Wicca the most. Wiccans have a creed and specific way of practice. They do not believe in harming others with magick and do not practice any "dark" spell work.

First, you are asked to pick a god and goddess to work with. I didn't believe in spirits or gods but was trying to play by the rules, so I looked into it. You could choose any of them from any Pantheon. I decided that if they turned out to be real, I would want to work with the gods of knowledge.

One book I read recommended that you be more open to gods who would approach you first, lest you try to choose to work with a particular god and he or she reject you. It also warned that these beings would not work with you for free and that you should expect to give something to them, even if it is just your time promoting that god to other people.

As instructed, I called out to the gods, letting them know I was looking for someone to work with. I sat and waited. It wasn't but one minute that passed before I felt a presence in the room. This was a familiar, relaxing, loving presence. I knew this was the God I grew up with. I was open to the idea of spirits, but I did not believe in Christianity and had no idea why God was approaching me like this.

Something told me, "This must be a trick of the mind. You are used to thinking God feels like that, so that must be why you feel this presence. Even if He is real, the stories you were told about Him weren't. Maybe He is just one of many spirits out there you can work with. Why work with this jealous one?" After listening to a lot of the Atheistic arguments in the past on how the God of the Bible, if real, is a mean and angry God, why would I want to work with Him?

I felt conflicted and told Him no. I wanted to work with someone else. I didn't want to have anything to do with a belief system that I didn't understand how to make work. Besides, I was here to experiment with Wicca and determine if magick worked. You aren't allowed to get involved with magick in Christianity.

> *"There shall not be found among you anyone who burns his son or his daughter as an offering, anyone who practices divination or tells fortunes or interprets omens, or a sorcerer or a charmer or a medium or a necromancer or one who inquires of the dead, for whoever does these things is an abomination to the Lord..."* (Deuteronomy 18:10-12)

After I told Him no, I felt the warm presence leave. I waited to see if any others would come. As I was told would happen, names and images of a few gods and goddesses came to mind, but I wasn't interested in them. I decided to work with the ones I had in mind, which I will not mention here.

I looked online for advice from people who worked with those specific gods. I learned what these particular gods liked and would respond to. No matter how hard I tried, though, I could not get them to respond to me. Was it because they weren't real? I wasn't sure.

I looked up what people should do if they couldn't find gods to suit them. Apparently, you could choose "feminine energy" and "masculine energy," calling these The Goddess and The God. Goddess energy was represented by the moon, and god energy was represented by the sun. It worked out better for me that way anyway because many classic Wiccan-written stories and materials just used the titles "The Goddess" and "The Horned God."

I went through a Wiccan dedication ritual and dedicated myself and my practice to the god and goddess. I felt a new presence with me during it. It was creepy, to be honest, especially because I still wasn't sure I believed in these things, yet I felt something there.

The process involved candles, expensive oils, incense, and a few "witchy" materials. I found it interesting that in several older traditions, including some Christian practices, sometimes dedications involved a type of oil on the forehead drawn in a specific symbol. I've seen this in Christianity with olive oil or frankincense drawn in the shape of a cross on the forehead. In this Wiccan practice, frankincense was used to draw the symbol of the horned god (similar to a sun with horns) on the forehead and the goddess (similar to a full moon with crescent moons on each side) over the heart.

Now that I had finished the dedication process, it was time to do more shopping. I spent a few hundred dollars on witchcraft materials, including crystals, more incense and oils, candles of different colors, a small altar set up, tarot cards, a wand, and a small crystal ball. I liked my set-up; it looked as magical as it was supposed to be. There were lots of pleasant smells and beautiful Celtic designs with many mysterious symbols.

I picked up a book on using Tarot cards and immediately tried it. You can use these cards in a few ways, but to keep it simple, I was using them in a way that was supposed to give me more immediate answers so that I could see the results quickly.

The first few times I tried the cards, they didn't work well. The answers were also very vague, and as a skeptic, I did not care for that at all. The books I read said that, at first, the answers may not be very accurate. They explained that the cards needed to be endowed with more of your energy first, so you were encouraged to hold them and envision moving energy from your body into the cards. I decided to give it some more time, so I chose to be patient about it.

Next, I tried candle magick. I was instructed to take a candle whose color matched my intentions and carve specific words or symbols into it. I also put an essential oil on it and set it up in a particular space. After setting it up, I was supposed to light the candle and visualize the outcome I wanted while staring at the flame. I focused on the flickering light and used my imagination to see everything play out a certain way.

After doing that, depending on the spell you were using, you could let the candle burn down or blow out the flame and imagine the energy of what you just visualized going out into the universe. It's just like what we are told to do on a birthday. "Make a wish and blow out the candle!" In the case of spell work, though, you needed to believe it would happen and behave like it would happen. This idea is a fundamental belief in all things New Age. Visualization and believing that what you see will come to pass at some point.

There is a bit of psychology at play here. Let's say that you want to build muscle and become strong. You picture yourself, with as much detail as possible, working out, eating right, and lifting 200 pounds over your head. Next, you start to behave in the ways you see that future version of yourself behaving. You already pictured in detail how that would go. So, you would start working out, eating right, and acting more confidently.

Tada! With a bit of time and patience, you get the results you were looking for, but was it because of magick and spirits? Or was it because the steps you are required to take for the spell to work ask for a change in mindset and behavior? Many New Agers argue it is a combination of both. As for my candle experiments, they didn't work out very well. I didn't get any of the results I was looking for, so it was onto the next type of spell work…

I had a tiny cauldron sitting on my altar. That's right, some witches actually do use cauldrons, but they aren't usually the huge kind you typically see in movies. This one was the size of a baseball. There is a particular time during the moon phases in which witches are encouraged to let things go.

Choosing to do spells during the correct moon phase was important because the spells were more likely to work during these times. Moon energy was a big thing in Wicca. It was goddess energy, and Wicca placed great importance on goddess energy.

I thought of something I wanted to let go and wrote it on a small piece of paper. I took that paper, placed it in the cauldron, read a spell, and lit the paper on fire. As I watched it go up in flames, I thought about how freeing it felt. I wasn't sure if it would work, but I enjoyed the process.

You may have been to Christian camps that have done something similar. I know I have. You write down something on paper you want to place in God's hands, light the paper on fire, pray to Him, and ask for His help with the problem. So, how effective was this magick? The spell didn't do anything, but burning something and letting go can be beneficial psychologically.

Time went by as I experimented with different kinds of magick. I didn't see any results that couldn't be explained away, but I did notice some other unusual things...

First Contact

I was sitting on the couch, completely focused on the video game I was playing when I felt someone come up behind me. I paused my game and turned around, but no one was there. "Strange..." I thought. I listened for a moment but didn't hear anything. I was the only one in the house at the time. I turned back to my game and started playing again.

This would happen to me over the course of a week. It felt like someone was following me, but it only happened while I was in the house. I started to wonder if I was finally getting some spirit contact, but I also reminded myself that there was a chance that things like that didn't exist and that I shouldn't make any conclusions without something solid to work with.

Rather than treat the god and the goddess passively like I had been up to this point, something told me I should start actively giving offerings, as my witchcraft books had recommended. I looked up what other Wiccans and Pagans were doing and began mimicking them.

On my altar, I offered things like water, olive oil, bread, flowers, etc. I also began celebrating pagan holidays, such as Yuletide,

Halloween, Equinox times, etc. I would follow the traditional practices of those holidays and feel like a part of something bigger because of it.

On one occasion, I can't remember if it was Halloween or Yuletide, I created a salt circle and set up two candles: a black candle to represent the goddess and a white candle to represent the god. I followed the instructions of lighting each candle and inviting only friendly spirits into my circle as I read the tale of the god and goddess out loud.

In the spring, the goddess gave birth to the god. In the summer, the god became very strong, and he and the goddess became lovers. She became pregnant. In the fall, the god's power weakened, and he knew he would die soon, leaving his pregnant lover. As the god died, everything became silent with winter as the goddess wept, but when she gave birth in the spring, she gave birth to the god ("Wheel of the Year"). The cycle of birth and death would be repeated year after year...

As I read out loud the part about the god dying, the "god" candle started melting quickly till it was almost ready to burn out. The goddess candle stood as tall as it did before. They were placed right next to each other, and there wasn't any reason this should have happened. I began to recognize the presence of different energies in my circle. "Are the gods trying to interact with me?" I pondered. My skeptic wall was starting to crack, but I needed more than this experience to be sure.

I noticed that the more attentive I was to my altar, the more interactions I started to get. Things like animals leading me to places with more of the witchcraft materials I was looking for, strange things happening with the candles I anointed, energies revealing themselves as spirits trying to teach me the ways of the spirit realm, etc. Once these spirits revealed themselves to me, I could not deny their existence anymore. I finally got what I asked for. I now started calling myself a Wiccan.

I can look back and see what their process was... Initially, when I was first trying to get an interaction, I only wanted it so I could know the spiritual realm was real and choose to side with the God of the Bible. The one true God. The spirits only started giving me proof after I truly rejected God. I had to dedicate myself to them and hear what they had to say about God first to make sure that, even if I did believe He could exist, I wouldn't want to work with Him. They made God look like someone you would never want anything to do with and made themselves look like friends of humanity.

While my husband and I were still dating, I went to church several times with him. I hadn't been inside a church for a while, but I thought I would go to show him that I supported him in his faith.

I didn't pay much attention to the sermons, but I enjoyed some of the friendly people, the atmosphere, and the occasional church potluck lunch. I had kept the promise I made him and would take time to say a quick "Please be with Zack" to God, but that was the extent of attention I would give to Him.

I started joining forums and groups for Wiccans and other Pagans. There were many "Christian Wiccans" out there, which I found to be surprising. I made friends with some of them. We would talk about our experiences with our spirit guides. They recommended better communication through a process called Astral projection.

Astral projection, also called astral travel, is a term used to describe an intentional out-of-body experience through which consciousness can function separately from the physical body and travel through a place called the astral plane.

The astral plane is the realm of the non-physical. It is part of our realm but the part we cannot see. It is the place where spirits, both good and evil, exist. People from many parts of the world have been doing this for thousands of years.

Some even quote Paul and say that he spoke of astral projection.

> *" I know a man in Christ who fourteen years ago was caught up to the third heaven—whether in the body or out of the body I do not know, God knows. 3 And I know that this man was caught*

up into paradise—whether in the body or out of the body I do not know, God knows— 4 and he heard things that cannot be told, which man may not utter.." (2 Corinthians 12:2-4).

Many sources claim that the soul is attached to the body by a white thread and that the soul can leave the body through astral projection.

I wanted to learn more about the spiritual realm by traveling it, so I researched how to astral project. As I researched, I saw many warnings about this practice. Many people would talk about how traveling there leaves your soul open to spiritual attacks by evil spirits. Some would tell stories about leaving their bodies and being able to look down and see themselves or even family members in different rooms. There was a claim that the CIA would hire people who were good with astral projection to assist them in finding the people they were looking for (Pruitt).

Others would talk about running into demons on the astral plane who would harass and begin oppressing them, even after they returned to their bodies. If these experiences were true, the risks seemed great. Did great risks ever stop me before? Absolutely not. Knowledge of the truth has always been worth it to me.

I prepared myself for this travel and followed the instructions on how to do it. Actually, I tried many times. Why? Because it didn't work. I wanted to go there, but I couldn't. I wondered if the people who say they are astral projecting were just imagining things...

After about a year of practicing Wicca, I stopped practicing many spells and served the gods less. To be honest, the spells were a lot of work for not a lot of results, and a lot of things in life were pulling my attention away from the gods.

The conclusion I drew from my Wiccan practice was that there is definitely a realm of energy beings (spirits) out there. We can't see the wind, but we can experience it and sometimes harness its power. I believed these beings were not all bad and were not all good, and you could interact with them or choose to ignore them. I believed that, as with many things discovered, science would one day have more to back these things up.

Psychologically, looking at the color red can cause your heart rate to go up, and the smell of lavender can have calming effects on people (Cherry). Once upon a time, people might have heard those statements and brushed it off as superstition but now we can see that these things are true and proven. I figured science would one day prove that these "energy beings" existed, too.

I was beginning to see how different energies flowed through the universe. Some were conscious energies (spirits), and others flowed unconsciously. What details did I believe about these things? I wasn't sure. I became very Agnostic in my beliefs but leaned Wiccan in my understanding of the world.

I had a quote by Riitta Klint on many of my decorations and cups that I loved at the time. Maybe you have heard its first sentence before, not really knowing what it meant.

> *"Stay wild, moon child. I will shine my full silver light on your path, Moon child. Trust your intuition and follow your dreams. When I go dark, go within and tend to yourself, set your goals and release what no longer serves. When I come out of the shadow Moon child, go, be brave, and to yourself stay wild and true."*[5]

This quote explains the kinds of magick that are most effective during a new moon (inner) versus a full moon (outer). Many witches obsess over the moon as it represents goddess energy and is important for spell and energy work. At one point, I even wanted to get a tattoo of the goddess moon symbol on the back of my neck. I'm so glad I didn't…

> We were called children of the goddess. A Moon Child.
> I followed the moonlit path to a new practice…

It's Just Exercise, Right?

A Descent into Yoga

> "Yoga is not just an exercise system. Yoga is the science of obliterating the boundaries of individuality to know the universality of one's existence."[1]
>
> SADHGURU

I DECIDED IT WAS time to start focusing on getting healthier and fitter. After several years of exploration and experimentation with different belief systems, I wasn't happier or calmer. I had started stress eating and felt like I needed to lose a few pounds.

A Christian university nearby offered workout classes cheaper than some gyms. I went to see what they offered and found myself signing up quickly. They had everything from swimming classes to Pilates to dance workouts. I picked a class, went, and had a blast.

I spotted yoga on the workout list and decided to try it. The only experience I had with yoga was those YouTube videos I followed along with a couple of years back. I thought it would be a good way to get fit and flexible while also relieving some stress.

My favorite classes ended up being the yoga classes. They involved breathing exercises called Pranayama, Asanas (yoga poses), and a practice at the end of the class in which you relax all of your muscles while lying on the ground trying to empty your mind (Savasana). The last portion of the class was trying to teach you a type of meditation.

At this point, I attended yoga classes regularly and almost exclusively. It made me feel powerful in my mind and body. I remember lying in that last meditation several times, feeling my "connectedness" to everything in the universe. It felt like a spiritual experience.

One day, after a class, the yoga instructor approached me. She was a lovely woman who cared a lot about people. She told me I was very good at yoga and asked me if I had ever considered teaching it. I hadn't, but I was trying to figure out what I would like to do as a career. Teaching yoga sounded like a great option; it was something I really loved practicing, after all. I told her I would look into it.

I searched for schools and found a yoga college nearby. It was also very affordable, so I was excited to get started. I waited a couple of months for the fall semester program to start.

When I pulled up to the school for the first time, I saw many people outside waiting for the door to open. Some were dressed in sports attire like I was. Others were dressed in stereotypically "hippie" clothing, and some wore things with symbols I recognized from witchcraft or Christianity.

They asked us to remove our shoes at the entrance and place our bags in the cubbyholes nearby. I had pictured a place with desks, a whiteboard, and yoga mats, but this place was just like a regular yoga studio. I felt a little silly because of my assumption of the place and brushed off my expectations, realizing that I had no idea what was involved in teacher training at a yoga college.

We were asked to grab our mats and pick up a Mexican blanket from the back room. When folded up, we were told those blankets make great meditation seats. I chose a spot in the room, rolled out my mat, placed my folded Mexican blanket down, and sat on it.

After going around the room introducing ourselves, we were handed binders called our Teacher Training Manuals. My guess was that it would contain a curriculum involving mostly anatomy and exercise rules. When I opened it, the first thing it said we would be learning was how to lead an "Om" chant.

> *"Spirit has brought us together and our collective spirit can be experienced most yogically in relationship to the Absolute. Another word for the Absolute is Om.."*[2]

That was a quote from the Program Structure in my manual. It goes on to say, *"Om is yoga."*[2]

I brushed off a lot of what was written about spirituality because I thought I was there to learn how to teach exercise and stretching. Due to my more Wiccan views of things at this time, I didn't find anything that was being said a problem; it was just a different point of view on the universe.

The program schedule categories included:

- Chants (each session had a specific sacred mantra).
- Teacher Perceptions (teaching ideas).
- Main Poses (learning to teach poses).
- Energy Experiencing Techniques (we were told these would be safer than tantric techniques).
- Yogic Biological Science (Yoga Anatomy and Ayurveda).
- Yogic Religiosity (Yogic ideas credited to a superhuman force).
- Consciousness Level (Samadhi, Dyana, Darana, Pratyahara, and Pranayama).
- Program Practices (Practicing what was taught in the lesson).

If you don't understand what all those terms explaining consciousness level mean, understand they come from Hindu thought on how to become one with Brahman, or what they were calling in my class to be inclusive of other religions, the Absolute. I never heard the name Brahman mentioned once in my classes.

Yoga means to yoke. I am sure some of the Christian students attending would have thought twice about these classes if they were being told they were trying to yoke themselves with a Hindu god called Brahman.

Another term I used above was Ayurveda. Ayurveda is an alternative medicine system from India based on "energies." Our manual also briefly discussed the Chakra system.

As I look over my manual now, I see something I underlined.

"Our hearts can communicate with other hearts, not just through abstract consciousness, but through electro-sensory impulses that can cause heart-cells from two different hearts to beat in unison (in laboratory tests)."[2]

This was stated right under the section on chakra, and that is important. I could sweep all the other spiritual-sounding stuff under the rug, but I trusted science, and this is just one example of some of the things I learned that made me wonder if there was something to stuff like the Chakra system. I know now that these laboratory tests did not have anything to do with chakra, but due to where it was placed in my manual, I couldn't quite see that at the time.

The manual presents Yamas and Niyamas, which are like a code of ethics. The five Yamas are non-violence, truthfulness, non-stealing, sexual continence, and non-greediness. The five Niyamas are cleanliness, contentment, discipline, self-study, and surrender to a higher power.

When I first read these, I agreed with many of them but didn't know what to do about the last niyama. I didn't have a god with a name to worship and respect. I decided yoga didn't have to be spiritual and that these things should be optional, so I decided to practice the last niyama by respecting "energies," whatever or whoever they might be.

I didn't have a code of ethics at this time besides the wiccan rede to not harm others, so I thought it would be fun to discipline myself by trying to follow these yamas and niyamas.

In the back of my manual was a list of requirements needed to graduate. 120 hours of class time, 40 hours of regular public yoga classes, 4 hours of yoga workshops, 4 hours at spiritual music concerts, 4 hours at meditation seminars, 20 hours assisting at a public yoga venue, reading all required books (things like the yoga sutras and yogic anatomy books), and finally, to teach at least 3 classes. Once you have completed all of the above requirements and graduated, you will have completed the requirements by the Yoga Alliance to become a registered yoga teacher.

Classroom Experiences

I had many experiences going to school; a lot of them were great, and some of them were not so great. As I got to know the other students attending school with me, I realized I had surrounded myself with people of many different paths: Buddhists, Taoists, Agnostics, Christians, Hindus, and many others. They were all very lovely people who were easy to get along with.

We had two instructors: an older husband and his wife. The wife was so sweet and had much love to share with everyone around her. The primary instructor was a funny guy who had a passion for making a difference in social and political injustice. Everyone got along very well.

Some days, during our lunch breaks, I would walk down the street with some of my new friends and grab a bite to eat. We would talk about our experiences in life and many spiritual things. I was asked many questions about how magick worked, as I called myself Wiccan then. When I explained it as energy work, some compared it to practices in yoga. I hadn't thought of it like that, but yes, yoga was like moving energies on the inside; at least, that was my understanding of it at the time.

When talking to some of my Christian friends about how they felt about the mystic side of yoga, some of them would write it off, saying they believed what the Bible said, not Hindu thought. Others would say we couldn't really understand how God works, so this could be another way to relate to Him, and it was okay to be involved in yoga if they believed the story of Jesus and still went to church. Some would say that they were still considering how they felt about it. Being surrounded by yogic philosophies and statues of other gods all day could certainly cause a person to question what they believed, so I understood what my friends were saying.

I remember the day that they introduced us to Kundalini yoga. Here is Kundalini, as defined by *Wikipedia*:

> *"...energy that lies within the body, frequently at the navel or the base of the spine. In normative tantric systems, kundalini is considered to be dormant until it is activated (as by the practice of yoga) and channeled upward through the central channel in a process of spiritual perfection."*[3]

verywellmind.com explains it's meaning a little better...

> *"In Hinduism, Kundalini is a form of feminine energy that is said to be coiled at the base of the spine. The word Kundalini comes from the Sanskrit word meaning "coiled snake." This energy can then be awakened through yoga, mantras, asanas, and meditation. Kundalini meditation is part of Kundalini yoga and is meant to move energy through the body. It is based on the concept that energy at the base of the spine (also known as the root chakra) needs to be released through the seven chakras of the body and then out through the crown chakra above the head."*[4]

The teacher warned us that Kundalini could be a dangerous practice if done wrong, so he would only introduce us to the surface of what it offered. He told us that if we got uncomfortable, it would be fine for us to stop and watch.

We sat around the room in an oval shape with our legs crossed and the lights dimmed. He proceeded to teach us a Kundalini breathing technique called Breath of Fire. It looks like hyperventilating, but it is more controlled than that. If you do it wrong, you could end up dizzy or numb. We were doing this because of chakra work, which we hadn't learned much about previously in class.

Before we began, the teacher explained that there are chakra points that follow the path of our spine. He told us that unlocking our chakra points allows the Kundalini energy to work its way up. He explained that blocked or overactive chakra points are one of the reasons we have certain health problems, so it is to our benefit to unblock those points.

As we started the Breath of Fire practice, I became very uncomfortable, as he said could happen. It felt like a heavy energy was coming upon me. Also, like the teacher said could happen, I began to feel anxiety. As a heavy skeptic, I wasn't sure this practice would do anything anyway, so I stopped and decided to sit and watch.

A few other students started to get dizzy and experience anxiety as well, so I watched them give up on the exercise. Some students started crying, and some started shaking. I began to feel very uncomfortable with the energy in the room as I watched. This experience and the pseudoscience of chakras were the first indications that I may have gotten into something quite abnormal.

We once did a type of meditation practice. The kind lady instructing us that day was there as a guest and teaching an optional event. I was getting better at my yoga practices, and it made me feel powerful and capable. I wanted to get even better, so I thought training my mind with a meditation practice would be beneficial.

We sat cross-legged in a circle, and she asked us to pick a deity to visualize for this practice. Some of the Christians around me chose Jesus. I closed my eyes and decided to see who came to mind. An image of Ganesha came up, the Hindu god I remembered from the temple I visited. I gained respect for Ganesha, so it isn't a surprise that he came to mind. I focused on his image while meditating for about 30 minutes.

Afterward, I felt I had made a deeper spiritual connection with myself and his image. When I focused on him, I heard in my mind,

"All gods are the same in the Absolute." I thought, "Wow, maybe when we were in the room, thinking of Buddha, Krishna, Jesus, and others, we were all thinking of the same force." I thought it could be possible. Even before this experience, I had some of these thoughts just by practicing yoga. While loud at first, my mind learned how to quiet as I went from pose to pose. Yoga, after all, is called a moving meditation.

As I went through the rest of my teacher training, I started to consider things I thought were silly before, such as "Oneness with the Universe" and chakras. My Wiccan practices had prepared me to feel different energies in the universe, so it isn't surprising.

By the end of this time, a lot of my Christian friends had started using Angel cards (like Tarot but trying to get answers from angels instead), crystal work, chakra work, trying to understand truth in meditation, and some even had statues of other gods in their houses. To this day, some of them still call themselves Christian while contacting different spirits, practicing divination, and worshiping other gods alongside the God of the Bible. It's interesting just how much yoga can change a person.

When I finally graduated, I was thrilled! I was thrilled to start teaching but also sad to leave because I had enjoyed the school so much. Yoga made me feel more confident in my abilities, and I wanted to teach others how to get there. I didn't continue meditating or practicing any of the spiritual sides of yoga. I wanted to teach it as exercise only. Most studios you go to don't do things like chanting; instead, they try to present yoga as an exercise for body and mind.

I had been to many yoga studios, and as a teacher, I could hear and spot how these teachers were trying to get their students into different frames of mind. I could hear how they would throw in a little mystic thought here and there. Some were more open about what they were doing, while others would use wording to disguise the metasciences they were teaching to sound more agreeable.

While some teachers were quieter about what they were trying to get you to do, they did it out of good intentions. They believe they have a level of awareness that their students don't have yet, and they are just trying to help the students achieve it. They do not have bad intentions, and I do not want to portray yoga teachers as manipulative people. A lot of them are wonderful people who want to help others.

I know a few Christian yoga teachers are reading this and thinking, "Well, I teach a Christianized version of yoga, so we sing hymns instead of chants, worship God instead of Brahman while doing yoga, and do Son Salutations instead of Sun Salutations." I will write more on this topic as my story progresses, but if you want to see why there is no such thing as "Christian yoga" right now, I have the answers in the chapter titled *"And Then He Spoke."* I recommend reading through the other chapters first for a more in-depth understanding.

A Small Window

I don't remember all the details of this particular experience I am about to share with you, but it is important to include this in my written story. It was one of the rare days I decided that I wanted to go to church with my boyfriend. I was bored as I sat in the pew listening to all the music, announcements, and scripture reading. My time in the yoga studio around Christians made me more accepting of their path. They showed me that Christians were not what I had been stereotyping, and some were more open in their spiritual path than I thought they could be.

The pastor came up onto the stage. He said his sermon today would be for Christians who forgot how to be Christian and for people who were not Christian. He titled the sermon *"Back to the Basics."* Something happened as I was listening. I was trying to write off what he was saying, but then God, loudly and warmly, made His presence known to me. His presence was overwhelming. At this point in my life, I was more familiar with spiritual beings and could easily recognize this one.

At the end of this sermon, the pastor invited anyone who felt moved by God's spirit to take a small card in the pockets of the pews and write their name and the date on it. I was touched that God was still asking me to be in a relationship with Him. Unlike any other spirit I had worked with, He emanated pure love. I wrote my name on one, holding the tears back while feeling the conflict inside, and put it in my wallet. What did this mean? Why was God doing this?

I called myself Christian at this point because this is the setting where He made Himself clearer to me. I didn't know what to think of Jesus or the Bible. I just knew that God was real and that He wanted me to know that. Maybe He was the "Absolute" I learned about in school? Was He the one behind all belief systems? I wasn't sure...

Introduction to Marijuana

After I graduated, I realized that most places hiring yoga instructors want you to be certified in more than one thing. I took another year and got certified as a personal trainer. Covid hit soon after, and because of that, all the gyms closed. I didn't know what to do. I couldn't teach now. Most everywhere in that part of California was in lockdown, and most of us had to stay home. I kept up at home with yoga so I wouldn't lose my flexibility.

One day, someone I know came to visit. Now, I know I was living in California, where marijuana is legal, but I had never thought to try the stuff. They brought a bag of it in an edible gummy form. I'm not sure what made me think of trying it; maybe it was just the thrill of a new experience, so I asked if I could have some. I would have the occasional sip of alcohol, but I had never tried anything like this.

It wasn't anything like what I had imagined it to be. For some reason, maybe because of media, I thought you might see things when you are high on this stuff, but you don't. I wouldn't say I liked it very much the first time. I accidentally had too much, so I didn't enjoy the experience. I thought I would never try it again, but someone else convinced me to try it again.

The second time, I enjoyed it much more. I felt very relaxed and giggly. I thought, "Maybe I will just do this every once in a blue moon." It went from occasional to "Weekends only. I wouldn't want to be irresponsible and do it more often." From there, I found myself doing it most days of the week until, eventually, it was every night.

They tell you this stuff is not addictive, so I was willing to try it. I told myself, "Well since this is not addictive, I could stop whenever I want, so it's fine that I use it this much now." I had a lot of good times using it, but the more excessive my use was, the less the stuff worked and the more I had to spend on it.

I noticed that my ways of thinking started changing slightly, and I became more thoughtful about many things. What I hadn't noticed was that anxiety started creeping up on me during my use. It went from being something very chill and calm while using it to getting bad anxiety and becoming anti-social. I would still go back for more, though, because it gave me relief for the first part of the high.

Looking back, it is sad to think that so many of the intimate conversations I had and experiences are now forgotten. Part of getting really high on weed is forgetting some of the things that happened. I remember some of it, but I wish I could remember more.

I became depressed and stressed out. Knowing I wasn't doing the job I had gone to school for yet, having to be in the house all the time due to Covid, and other experiences, all contributed to the reason I had to numb out all those emotions by getting high. I think it calmed me in some ways, but in other ways, it made me more erratic. I did a lot of things I wasn't proud of at this time.

One thing I feel like I got out of using marijuana was that it brought down some of my emotional walls. I felt much more connected to the people around me and developed a lot of empathy. Because of this, I believed marijuana was bringing out the best in me. I see now it wasn't.

I "greened out" once. What that meant in my case was that I took so much marijuana in one setting that I got terribly sick and was throwing up. I was ill for a few days. I was nauseated every moment. I threw up several times a day, and the slightest smell of weed would make me want to throw up again. It was the sickest I had ever been at the time. It was a bit of a wake-up call for me. I decided to take a break from it for a while. I did, but I was back on it again after a while.

> Maybe it was time to get some help...little did I know that I was about to be exposed to a strange form of new-age in the world of "Self-Help"...

That Which You Think, You Attract

A Descent into "Self-Help"

> "I'm going to be happy. I'm going to skip. I'm going to be glad. I'm going to be easy. I'm going to count my blessings. I'm going to look for reasons to feel good. I'm going to dig up positive things from the past. I'm going to look for positive things where I stand. I'm going to look for positive things in the future. It is my natural state to be a happy person. It's natural for me to love and to laugh. This is what is most natural for me. I am a happy person."[1]
>
> ABRAHAM HICKS, AFFIRMATIONS

I MOVED FROM CALIFORNIA back to Tennessee after COVID-19 hit and started teaching yoga. I started with family members, then friends. I started gaining clients for regular gym training or yoga through some of them. I loved teaching yoga. I felt like it focused more on the mind-body-spirit connection.

Soon, through one of those connections I made, I was asked if I could lead a yoga studio that this person was trying to get set up. It would be one that the students could legally get high in on a form of marijuana called Delta-8. There would have to be a lot of work done first. Finding a space to rent, figuring out the legal stuff... I had plenty of time to prepare. I said yes, of course. It seemed like a rare opportunity to me, and I was excited!

Since I knew I would be running a studio soon, I decided I needed to become the best teacher I could be. I bought more yoga books, practiced the sequences more, and started looking up YouTube videos explaining how to run a successful business.

While searching for business advice, I stumbled across a young man who presented some new ideas to me. His name was Aaron, and he talked about mindset being everything. One of the first videos I saw of his was titled "*7 Habits that Made Me a Millionaire in 2 years.*" In basic, the habits were to go the extra mile, question your status quo, commit to a daily action that involves your vision, pattern recognition, meditation, expand the circle of who you talk to, master your morning routine, and do that highest leverage thing that brings you closer to your vision.[2] His advice seemed very good. It gave me the idea to investigate how successful business owners became successful. Who better to learn from than the people who actually reached those goals?

I noticed in many of his videos that he would talk about "changing your vibration" or "raising your vibration" and kept talking about a concept called the Law of Attraction. As I looked up other successful/famous people and what they were reading, many of them recommended the book titled *The Law of Attraction* as well.

I went to my local bookstore to search for it. Strange, I couldn't find it in the self-help section... I asked one of the employees if they could help me, and they took me to the New Age section. There it was, mixed in with the spell books and tarot cards. I opened it up, confused as to why this highly recommended book was categorized as "New Age." I quickly saw why...

Esther Hicks, the author of the book, describes what she is doing as tapping into "infinite intelligence" to get the information she writes in her book. This "intelligence" is called Abraham. It consists of a group of entities that are channeled by Esther Hicks. Abraham described themselves as *"a group consciousness from the non-physical dimension."* They say, *"We are that which you are. You are the leading edge of that which we are. We are that which is at the heart of all religions."*[3]

The Law of Attraction states that we attract things into our lives according to our thoughts. Whatever we place our thoughts upon, we will attract more of. Positive thoughts bring positive experiences, and negative thoughts bring negative experiences.

When I read about the entity called Abraham, my first thought was that the Christians I knew would probably have thought this was someone who was possessed by demons. The concept of the Law of Attraction seemed to be correct, though. That may be why so many successful people used it to get where they were. Looking back, this is what makes many of these New Age ideas easy to fall into; they have some truth to them.

Before leaving the bookstore, I noticed a set of yoga-based oracle cards in the New Age section. They had pictures of many Hindu gods and yogic concepts on them. I picked them up for a closer look and saw they were supposed to accompany a yoga journal. I hadn't messed with Oracle or tarot cards in a while, but I liked these ones. You were supposed to draw a card, which would give you advice for that day or tell you what to expect.

I hadn't had much success with tarot cards, but these could be more practical as they could give me something to focus on each day. I ordered the journal that went with it as well. I liked how the journal would provide you with a yogic theme each month to focus on and a card drawing to tell you how to reach that goal. It had a daily section where you would draw your daily card, journal things you were grateful for, and write down the highlights of your day.

As the days went by, I began teaching more and really started understanding the "vibrations" stuff. I noticed that as I took the advice from the *Law of Attraction* to just focus on joy, more joy started to form. I would focus more on the positive and seemed to attract the positive.

As I became more joyful, goal-focused, and spiritual, I started "attracting" people with similar qualities into my life. The "Law" states that this outcome happened because I was emitting those kinds of vibrations. When you send out a type of vibration, it attracts things, situations, and people who are a "vibrational match" to you.

I continued to read more books and listen to more speakers on success. Many of them were speaking about becoming a vibrational match to what they wanted. They were not using the term "vibration," though. They were trying to teach people about the Law of Attraction without calling it by name. I came to understand that they spoke in this undercover way because people would be more likely to listen to the concepts they were trying to teach.

After I came to accept the Law of Attraction, I was ready to hear what else Aaron had to share in his videos. He would say things about how after you came to the "realization" of specific topics, such as the Law of Attraction, you "vibrate" at a higher level and can see the world more clearly. He inspired me to stop doing things that would "lower my vibration," like drinking alcohol or holding on to anger. I felt like I was becoming a better and happier person, so I figured he must understand a lot.

He started uploading videos like "*3 Spiritual Awakening Traps that will Lower Your Vibration*" and "*4D Energies that are Influencing Your Life and You Don't Even Know It.*" What is 4D, you might ask? Well, the 3D world is the world of the physical, the illusion that you see in front of you every day. 4D and 5D are the stuff you don't see. The "energies" all around you. His message became more focused on how to "raise your vibration" enough to start "living in 4D or 5D."

It is true that what you see in front of you isn't all there is. Yes, there is a "spiritual realm," and even scientifically speaking, you can't see everything that is going on. Let's also look at the "*Spiritual Awakening*" in that first video title. That is of crucial importance. I noticed that once you reach a certain level in the self-improvement world, it all leads to some "spiritual awakening" teaching.

Whether you are listening to Aaron, Oprah, Tony Robbins, or Eckhart Tolle, they are all trying to eventually get you to "awaken" to this "reality" of 4D and 5D and not just give you some self-improvement advice. Once you "awaken" to that, you start noticing just how many of these big-name speakers, actors, and CEOs are "spiritual" in some way.

I have also seen how some people believe in this stuff and try to use it for evil. They don't want "the masses" to wake up to anything spiritual. They want them to remain ignorant cash cows. I felt like I was becoming more powerful and "energetically" aware. I felt like I was untouchable and started feeling like I had a calling to "wake people up." I didn't want the people I knew to continue to feel negative emotions. I didn't want the government and big businesses to take advantage of them. I wanted them to wake up to what I started to see as "reality" so that they could become powerful and have more control of their lives.

Some people I looked up to started talking about how our souls existed before this and that we chose to be here now. They said this era was special because we were moving into "the Age of Aquarius." This age is supposed to be when more of humanity starts waking up to "energetic truths" and slowly starts coming out of the "3D" experience.

We chose to be here; we agreed beforehand on what we would experience, who our family members would be, and what we would do here. This was said to be the hard truth. Why would you have chosen the bad experiences? What if you were abused? Did you choose that too? The explanation was that people who go through hard things like that are more likely to wake up faster and grow spiritually in ways others might not. "There cannot be growth without difficulty." That is a true statement. It is also true that a lot of the people in these "movements" had been abused or had experienced bad lives.

The *Law of Attraction* tells you that if something bad happens to you, it is because you attracted it by your thoughts and what they were focused on. If good happens to you, you attract it by focusing on good. The above explanation that you chose what would happen to you here on earth for spiritual growth also puts destiny into your own hands. Things feel less out of control. Everything has purpose and meaning. They say that you assign meaning to the things in your life. If you take a bad situation and say it was bad, it will affect you as such. If you take that situation and assign a good meaning to it, like saying you grew because of it, you have now turned it into a "good" situation. I now understand this to be what we call perspective.

A Mixed-Up Truth

First off, let's talk about the truths we can find in these teachings. The Law of Attraction encourages a person to think positively about their situations to bring about positive outcomes. Envisioning your goals being accomplished and doing what is necessary to bring that result about. If you have a goal and are unsure you will reach it, it will be harder to reach, right? Self-doubt is a destroyer of goals. But what if you believed with all your heart that you would reach it? The likelihood of you reaching that goal is much higher! It's also a lot easier to keep at it when you see situations positively. When you are being negative about things, you are dragging yourself down and are more likely to give up. You don't need the Law of Attraction to tell you these things. This is just common sense.

So, what is wrong with the Law of Attraction? There are many things I can list here, but let's look at some quotes from an article titled "*The Truth About the Law of Attraction*" from Psychology Today on the matter:

> "Don't get involved with anything negative like charity or helping the needy. This will attract more negativity and poverty. Wallace Wattles, an LOA founder, wrote, 'Do not talk about poverty; do not investigate it, or concern yourself with it. Do not spend your

That Which You Think, You Attract

time in charitable work, or charity movements, all charity only tends to perpetuate the wretchedness it aims to eradicate.' and 'Give your attention wholly to riches; ignore poverty.' Rhonda Byrne in The Secret takes this a step further: 'If you see people who are overweight, do not observe them…If you think or talk about diseases, you will become sick. What you think or surround yourself with — good or bad, is what you will bring upon yourself.' If you believe in LOA, avoid any of the "helping or health" professions such as physician, nurse, hospital worker, clergy, psychologist, police officer, paramedic, etc. Avoid professions in which you deal with poor people, such as accountant, mortgage broker, banker, lawyer. While research shows that charitable work, empathy, and volunteering are beneficial to both the giver and receiver, avoid these things if you believe in LOA."[4]

The article goes on to point out a few other good points…

"As the LOA is supposed to be a perfect, universal law, positivity should always attract more positivity. The corollary of this is that you alone are completely responsible for any goal that was not successfully achieved, no matter how unrealistic the goal. This assumes that you not only control your thoughts and actions, but also those of everyone around you…and nature. The fact is, you don't. Sorry to break that to you."[4]

"The only reason anything bad could ever happen to you is that you were thinking bad thoughts. If someone rear-ends you in a car — 100% your fault. If you get breast cancer — 100% your fault (not genetics). If you get raped or abused — 100% your fault. Children getting killed by terrorists, sick babies in the intensive care unit, victims of floods, hurricanes, natural disasters, the Holocaust — yes, their fault. We all know deep inside that this is ridiculous to even suggest. However, it is a basic, fundamental premise of the LOA. You never attract something you are not thinking about."[4]

Ok, so what about the idea that you chose what your experiences would be here on earth before you were born to grow spiritually? You came to this planet to learn something, right? You had to go through terrible things, such as abuse, in order to wake up faster and complete your mission here. You are told to let go and stop trying to control everything so you can progress to higher levels of awareness and let things "flow." Control is a "low vibrational" way of thinking.

If you believe this, I want to encourage you to keep an open mind to what I am about to say. Injustice is a terrible thing to deal with. It is easier to forgive and move on with life when you believe that whatever you went through had a much higher purpose and meaning. If you agreed to what was going to happen before you were born, then you were in complete control, and you still are. Having perceived control over our situations can cause us to feel better. But wait, aren't you supposed to be letting go of control? Hmm... there seems to be a contradiction here.

Childhood victims of poverty, abuse, trauma, mental disorders, bad parents, bullying, and such have a higher need for control to feel ok. Isn't it interesting that we are told that a lot of us who "wake up" to these ideas are people who have dealt with these types of problems growing up? This is not a coincidence. I hope you will think about what I am saying.

I was about to get a phone call that would drastically change the trajectory of my path...

Tat Tvam Asi – That Thou Art

A Descent into Hinduism

> "Hence men of wisdom should earnestly set about knowing the true nature of the Self."[1]
> VIVEKA CHUDAMANI

I WAS DOING WELL creating business plans for the future yoga studio. I even took time to practice yoga while high on marijuana to make sure I could teach students who would also be high on it. I made sure to be somewhat high while watching the "self-help" videos and "high vibe" videos to truly wrap my head around what was being said. At this point, I was also becoming a lot fitter. Everything seemed to be going well.

I was looking for a part-time job to make more money on the side while I was waiting for the studio to get put together. I saw that there was a Christian bookstore hiring nearby. I really loved the idea of being around books all day, even if it was in a Christian setting. I had called myself Christian for a little while now, but I wasn't sure what I actually believed. At this point, I thought that maybe the force that got my attention at church that day back in California was a true conscious force, but perhaps it was more of a "universal being" that people in many religions could understand.

One day, my grandmother called me. She wanted to talk to me about a book she was writing. She explained that she had learned some things about yoga that made it incompatible with Christianity and was writing a book about it. She said yoga was a Hindu worship practice.

She knew that I had been calling myself a Christian after my experience at church, but she didn't know that I didn't actually see the world the way most Christians did. To me, saying yoga was something Christians couldn't practice sounded silly. There are lots of Christians who practice yoga! They don't typically do chanting or chakra work, so I didn't see how a Christian couldn't participate. Many of my students were Christian and had no problem with it.

She gave me the contact information of a friend of hers who grew up in India and went to a Hindu school. He was trying to teach Christians the truth about yoga and why we shouldn't practice it. I knew I didn't believe the Bible in the way that she did, so I figured I wouldn't benefit from her friend's point of view either. I would reach out to him, but not yet.

When I taught yoga, I did not have my students chant or "Om." I didn't talk about anything mystical sounding to them either. I never saw the yoga I taught as anything that spiritual. From my viewpoint, you could separate Hindu yoga from what I called "Western yoga." It didn't have to be spiritual. It could just be exercise and stretching.

This whole matter caused me to go into a deeper study of yoga. I researched the definition of yoga and what its origins were. You might wonder, "If you went to school for yoga, wouldn't you know the answers to these questions already?" Yes and no. I knew that yoga stemmed from Hinduism, but I hadn't cared to look more into those origins because I didn't care about the spiritual side of things while I was in school. I am sure they went over some of this in class, but I tuned out a lot of the spiritual-sounding information while I was there.

Yoga is one of six orthodox schools of Hinduism. "If I am going to be the best yoga instructor, maybe I should be studying this school of Hindu thought more." When I did start studying it a little more, I saw that yoga teaches that ignorance is the cause of suffering. "Hmm... that's what I have been learning from Aaron. Living in 'higher vibrations' is having a greater awareness of 'reality.' Having greater awareness is causing me to suffer less. I am much happier than I have been in the past."

I had read some of Patanjali's *Yoga Sutras* while I was in school, but I figured if I was going to really get into yoga, I should study them. Yoga assumes the existence of God. I could accept this, as it really did seem that there was some force behind everything. Whether this was a conscious or an unconscious force, I wasn't quite as sure. In my circle of New Agers and Yogis, we just called this force the Universe.

Yoga says that spiritual liberation occurs when the spirit is freed from the bondage of matter. Matter causes ignorance and illusion. Someone who has learned to suppress and control the activities of the mind and has successfully ended attachment to material objects will be able to enter Samadhi.

Samadhi, sometimes called enlightenment, is a state of deep concentration that ends in a blissful union with the ultimate reality ("Samadhi"). This ultimate reality is God, the Universe, or Brahman, as Hinduism calls it. Whatever name you choose to use...

At this point, I started listening to Hindu swamis on YouTube explain these things in greater detail. Listening to their beliefs, I wasn't sure I could buy into them. Hinduism seemed far-fetched to me. I began wondering if I could be a good yoga instructor if I didn't believe in what yoga was all about. I wasn't ready to give up on it yet, though. I wanted to hear them defend why they could believe in any of these things. Besides, I could still teach it as an exercise, right?

One problem I noticed was that everyone I listened to kept repeating that before you even get into asanas, which are the yoga poses and the third stage of yoga, you were supposed to practice the first two stages. The first two stages are ethical preparations. The first step is Yamas (restraints), which are abstinence from violence, falsehood, stealing, lust, and being possessive ("Yamas"). The second step is the Niyamas (discipline), which includes cleanliness of the body, contentment, austerity, study, and devotion to God ("Niyamas").

These things would lead to better success at the yoga poses in the third stage. I wanted to practice these ethics the best I could. I saw these ethical practices as good things, so I took a deep dive into how to practice each very well.

I pulled out the yoga journal and Oracle deck I had purchased and began using them regularly. The journal encouraged me to call upon the energy of Brahman and other Hindu gods and goddesses. Unlike my tarot card readings, this yogic oracle deck would accurately predict daily occurrences. Not only that, but the force working through the cards also started to communicate things I needed to work on as an individual.

These communications were incredibly specific. Something was communicating with me, and whatever it was, it wanted me to stop existing as an individual and learn how to "become one with Brahman," whatever that meant.

Some New Agers I would listen to said that the "Universe" had another name. "Highest" or "Higher Self." This is Brahman as well. But what is Brahman? Brahman is the "supreme soul," the "universe," the creator. It is present in every atom of creation but remains there as the Viewer, not affected by creation. The individual soul is a part of Brahman, as everything is a part of Brahman.

I have heard it described in this way: According to the law of Conservation of Mass, matter is not created or destroyed. Brahman was the only thing in existence. It created everything, and every living thing has Brahman inside powering it ("Brahman"). Working our way through it backward, as the Swamis like to teach it, let's try to see from their point of view.

Who/What Am I?

The main principle is that "whatever I am aware of, I am not that." That which we are aware of is an "object" and not "awareness" itself. We have identified ourselves with things that are not our self, like the body or the mind. We call these "I" or "me." Hinduism teaches that we are not these; instead, we are pure awareness.

The "Seer" and the "Seen" are different. You are seeing this book right now and know that you and the book are different. You are not this book. You are the "Seer," and this book is the "Seen." When we hear, touch, taste, and smell, we always say, "I am the one who is seeing, hearing, and tasting." We are on the side of the experiencer. Our eyes see objects but cannot see themselves, right? We must have the reflective power of something like a mirror to see our eyes, but the eyes cannot actually see themselves. The eyes can only see something separate from themselves.

The eyes are something we also experience, though. The eyes, then, become the object. So, what is experiencing the eyes? The mind. Who registers all the incoming information from the eyes and thinks all the thoughts that come with that? The mind. It is observing the eyes, along with all the rest of your senses. Now the mind is the "Seer," and the body is the "Seen." "Seer" and "Seen" are different, right? The mind is different from the eyes.

Now, let's go even deeper. What is the mind? Thoughts, feelings, and emotions. But wait, we also experience these things, right? So, we must not be our thoughts, feelings, and emotions. We know our thoughts and feelings, so if these things are the "Known," then who is the "Knower"? We say, "I am experiencing the contents of my mind." Well, who is experiencing those contents? I am experiencing the contents of my mind, so I must not be my mind. Why? The "Seer" is not the "Seen."

Following this way of thinking, Hinduism says, "I am the Witness to my thoughts." You are the one witnessing your thoughts; thus, you are consciousness itself. Why are we calling this "consciousness"? It causes you to experience all these things; without it, everything would be blank. If your mind stops thinking and seems empty, you are still there, experiencing the emptiness. You are still aware of it. Even when thinking stops, awareness goes on. Hinduism says, "Rest in your nature, which is pure awareness ." That which experiences the body, mind, and intellect...that thou art.

Is that blankness nothing? Buddhists say yes. They believe in "the non-self." Hinduism says no. You are not a thing, but you clearly exist, so you are not nothing, either. You are consciousness and awareness, also described as soul.

Now, are you, as the consciousness, separate from the universe (everything we can experience)? Well, have you ever experienced the universe apart from your awareness? You cannot. All experience requires consciousness! Thus, there is no proof that consciousness is separate from the universe. Do you follow me so far? We are almost done...

Hinduism says the universe is an appearance in you. Consciousness is the reality, and the universe is an "appearance," an illusion. The universe is the dream of consciousness, the dream of Brahman. What is the "the hard problem of consciousness" science speaks of compared to "the hard problem of matter"? Consciousness is a reality that we experience all the time. The real mystery is matter. The more we investigate matter in physics, the more we realize we don't understand what matter is. From molecules to atoms to subatomic particles, to nuclei, sub-nuclear particles, to quarks, and now super-strings! What will be next?

I won't be explaining the entirety of the religion here. Like Christianity, there are different theologies in Hinduism, and not all Hindus agree with each other, but in this branch of Hinduism, the creator god Brahman is consciousness, and that is what you are at your core. Basically, Brahman is the only thing that really exists, and this creator god is "playing a game of hide and seek" with itself. There is a "fog" that keeps you from knowing who you are, and to "remember" is to reach enlightenment. If this is the case, then nothing you see is what you think it is. It is merely another form of

Brahman's illusion. There is also no death or reason to worry about anything if this is all just "you" anyway.[2]

If all of that seemed confusing, understand that even for a Hindu, this is supposed to take time to grasp. I was getting high on "Shiva's plant," cannabis, to understand these concepts better. The Hindu god Shiva is the supposed inventor of yoga, and many of his followers use cannabis. It's no wonder that so many in the yoga community use it.

Later, as I began to believe in this way of thinking, if someone hurt me, I remember thinking to myself, "It's okay. This is just a version of me that doesn't understand reality." Because of this way of thinking, no one could get to me, no one could hurt me, and I certainly didn't want to hurt anyone, knowing that they were just me but living a different experience.

The Buddha once asked a student, 'If a person is struck by an arrow, is it painful? If the person is struck by a second arrow, is it even more painful?' He explained, 'In life, we can't always control the first arrow. However, the second arrow is our reaction to the first. This second arrow is optional.' (Tanhane).

The moral of the story is that perspective and correct reaction to situations can change how much we suffer. When you accidentally spill your dinner all over the living room rug, this is the first arrow. However, if you become upset by this, feel angry, and start to complain, you hit yourself with a second arrow. While you can't control your circumstances, you can choose how to respond and choose to respond in a way that doesn't continue the hurt from the first arrow.

So what was the truth? It was time to get deeper into my yogic meditation practice to find out . . .

The Death of Self

A Descent into Meditation

"Meditation is not growth of the ego, it is death of the ego."[1]
RAJNEESH

I BEGAN MY MORNING routine with silent meditation in front of my Buddha and Ganesha statues. At first, I practiced with my eyes closed, but eventually, I tried to meditate with my eyes partly opened. I needed to see that what was in front of me was all just an illusion and not just understand it with my eyes closed.

I tried not to think of any thoughts. Thoughts were not who I was, and I needed to empty my mind to "get in touch" with the "real" me, that blankness behind the mind. It was a very peaceful, quiet way to start my day. After this, I would do a few Sun Salutations and practice the "moving meditation" that yoga is meant to be.

I was starting to connect more with my body and senses. I concentrated on living in and fully enjoying the present moment, which helped me appreciate life's simple pleasures more. Over time, if I did not start my day with these practices, I would feel very out of touch with things and more irritable.

After these practices, I would pull out my yoga journal and oracle cards. The force of "the universe" would give me clear and precise answers to guide me through my day. I recognized this "universe force" as Brahman or my Highest Self.

Occasionally, if I needed an entire conversation's worth of information, I would practice automatic writing. Maybe you have heard of this practice being used by spirit mediums? It is a similar concept. It is when you write down questions and allow a spirit to take over you and write the answers on paper.

In my practice, I knew that the answers were already inside me somewhere since "all was I, and I was all," in a sense. I would empty my mind, and the pen would start writing without me having to think of any thoughts. I would look away from the paper as the writing was happening to avoid getting distracted and start having thoughts again. I would feel something overtake me and start writing.

After it was done, I would look down and read the answers. The writing did not sound like me at all, so I knew this was something else trying to communicate with me. What was written down seemed like very wise and informative answers, and I was very satisfied with them. This "force" strategically led me deeper into Hindu understanding and successful ways of practicing it.

Next, before leaving to go to work at the Christian bookstore, I would do a walk-through meditation using one of Aaron's videos. I would usually lie down on my bed while listening to these videos. If I didn't work that day, I would use a little marijuana beforehand to help me concentrate on the meditation.

He would have me visualize being in a comfortable setting. Sometimes, it would be me sitting in front of a projector screen, asking my Higher Self to show me deep or lost memories from my childhood, maybe situations or people I needed to forgive. Sometimes, it would be ways to better myself, or he would try to take me on out-of-body experiences to the places where my spirit guides might reside to help me open chakras, which is very important for reaching enlightenment and oneness with Brahman.

During one of these sessions with Aaron, I felt the walls around my heart collapse. It was a very physical feeling. I thought this was my heart chakra opening fully. Any walls I had built up due to hurt and damage fell all at once, and I started to cry. I felt pure love for all those I knew and nothing but forgiveness for everyone.

The way I described this feeling to people was that it felt like what I would imagine demons being cast out of my body would feel like. I felt free. Free from the chains of hurt and unforgiveness. Free from seeing the world in a dark way. All I had was love and compassion overflowing inside of me. My heart was fully open to any and all living beings. I was a completely different person after that.

I would also take time to practice Kundalini yoga. Things started getting weird in my life after I regularly practiced it. As I mentioned in the chapter on my experiences in school, this form of yoga was told to be dangerous if you did it wrong. Ultimately, Kundalini yoga led to my major "spiritual awakening." Without it, I may not have reached a successful "yoking" with Brahman later.

After doing all this, I would go to work. I worked with many great people, and I loved my job. Being around books all day was a dream come true. My Christian friends at work did not realize that I was not actually a Christian. I identified myself as one, but I saw Christianity through the lens of a Hindu.

I remember trying to teach some of them yogic concepts, but in ways that I thought wouldn't sound threatening to their Christian walk. I learned how to do this by reading about Hindu yogis who came to the U.S.A. as Hindu missionaries. They knew this was a Christian nation, and so what they taught had to sound compatible with the Christian faith. Many came over wearing cross necklaces and would speak of how great Jesus was ("Christianity in India").

I even started teaching some of these new friends of mine yoga. I did not tell them what the purpose of yoga was. I told them that it was very healthy and was very good for helping them deal with stress and anxiety. I would slip in a few Hindu or New Age ideas here and there, but I don't think any of them could tell. I know I wouldn't have noticed it if I had been in their position. I wasn't trying to harm anyone, though. I was doing this hoping they would also one day be led down this path of "love and healing" I had found. I saw so much hurt and pain experienced by others, and I wanted to help people escape the pain.

One day, I decided to finally read a book I had meant to get to titled, "*Autobiography of a Yogi*," by Paramahansa Yogananda. It would be interesting to read the story of how someone from India became a yogi. I had not heard of Yogananda before this. Starting from his childhood, you see many supernatural things going on. He spoke of miracles and hidden knowledge of famous yogis in India that he had met. Everything from a teleporting man to a yogi who could levitate to people who mastered control of time and space. I was not expecting any of this from the book. It was very surprising to me. This was a book that many well-known people recommended and believed in. Steve Jobs himself read the book over 40 times ("Autobiography of a Yogi").

I went online to see if these kinds of miracles were common in India. They seemed to be something people knew of over there. Some people were faking miracles, but there were others, including Yogananda himself, who were said to have raised people from the dead ("Yogananda"). "Wow," I thought, "Are these things that people can do when they have mastered true yoga?" These were extraordinary claims. I wasn't sure if they were totally true, but I thought it could be possible.

In his other books on how to walk this spiritual path, Yogananda said many things I found to be very true and inspiring. I started really looking up to him. If I had read some of the things he wrote and told you these were from a sermon of a Christian pastor, you would have believed me. He was passionate about who he called the creator god and said he was Jesus's biggest fan. I found this to be interesting… I had not read the Bible in a long time and had not believed in Jesus, but here I was, reading about how a miraculous man such as Yogananda was saying that we should all be studying about Jesus and what he had said. I would give this some thought.

Deep in and Dying

Over time, I became very spiritual and got very good at meditation. My meditation practice had overtaken my yogic asana practices as I had come to learn that meditation was more important to reaching enlightenment.

I had an experience while meditating one day in which I successfully "merged" with the universe. I finally experienced being one with Brahman. This was not a state I constantly lived in, but I was working on it becoming that way. It happened while I was outside meditating one day. I was trying to "see reality how it truly was," according to Hindu thought, and then it happened. My thoughts disappeared, and I felt that looking through my eyes was like looking through a TV screen. It was not just me. I felt myself and another "being" looking through my eyes. Everything around me appeared fake and looked like an illusion to me.

If you have never experienced this, you may wonder what to think about this experience. It may sound like I finally lost my mind or that I had become partially demonically possessed. I now believe it was the latter. I want to point out that this state I experienced is exactly the goal of yogic Hinduism. It is the reason yoga exists. Yoga = to be yoked. To what? To Brahman. To destroy the "ego" is the only way. To destroy you. You should be very concerned about whether you are Christian or not. What are the consequences of such a practice? Let's go over just a few of the many consequences...

Depersonalization disorder is a big one. *Myclevelandclinic.org* explains it this way:

> *"In depersonalization-derealization disorder, you feel detached from yourself (depersonalization) and disconnected from your environment (derealization). While feelings like this may come*

and go for many people, in people with depersonalization-derealization disorder, they tend to last a long time (persist) or go away and come back (recur). Depersonalization affects your ability to recognize your thoughts, feelings, and body as your own. It might feel like you're watching yourself play a role in a movie rather than living your life. For example, if you're grocery shopping, you might feel like you're watching someone else push your cart, select food from the shelves, and go through the check-out line. Or you might not recognize your reflection in the glass doors of the frozen section. Derealization affects your ability to see your surroundings accurately. Things might not seem real. Or you might feel like you're looking through a clouded window or in black-and-white rather than full color. Objects might look distorted in shape or size, or you may feel like they change while you look at them. In depersonalization-derealization disorder, you may experience depersonalization, derealization or both. But you haven't lost touch with reality. You understand that your perceptions aren't real, which can be frustrating and cause anxiety. Psychiatrists classify depersonalization-derealization disorder as a dissociative disorder in the DSM-V."[2]

The leading causes of this disorder are things like physical abuse and extreme trauma, neither of which were things I was experiencing at the time. Isn't it strange that yogic meditation can and is supposed to lead to something like this state?

Another unfortunate effect of meditation like this is the destruction of ambition. Most people in my life have always known me to be a very ambitious person. I started losing ambition in almost every area of my life, though. Why? In the end, nothing out there was "real" or really mattered. Only becoming one with the universe so you could experience "truth" and see "reality" mattered. Ambition comes from the ego, so it is not something you want to possess. Letting go of all attachment was the goal, and ambition was the opposite. This would pacify you.

People are encouraged to meditate to help with anxiety, depression, anger, and many other things. It may help with these things for a little while, but after you become a long-term meditator and practice every day for a long time, all of this will backfire on you.

Many long-term meditators experience anxiety, anger, hopelessness, extreme depression, and many other things coming into their lives with a vengeance. This is said to be the "ego" trying to preserve itself and keep from dying. This means that these side effects are to be expected.

Don't just take it from me; I encourage you to listen to people who either used to practice or are still practicing this kind of meditation. They will tell you that if you are practicing meditation correctly, you will experience these miserable side effects, even if you had never experienced these things before starting your meditation practice.

"Weird" stuff should also be expected. Many of my yogi friends have experienced things like supernatural encounters during meditation, the urge to behave like an animal, strange body pains, the feeling of being possessed, etc. These are all very normal for long-term meditators. I am not saying that you will experience all of these things, but you will experience some of them.

Many of my friends and family members started noticing changes in me. Many would be in awe of my level of patience and understanding. Some would come to me for life advice, and "the universe" supplied me with information. For some reason, I knew things about their situations, thoughts, and feelings that they had not expressed to me. They were amazed at my " understanding " level, but this was not coming from me. In fact, ever since I quit these practices, I have not experienced this flood of information. In many of those moments, my "ego" would take the back seat, and this "universal being" would speak through me to them, and I would feel as if I were just watching it happen.

From the outside, I appeared to be very well put together, calm, and free from anxiety and dark thoughts. My family and friends had no idea how much I was "killing myself" from the inside. I was becoming hollow. My passions died. I was just a vessel. At least I wasn't experiencing the pains of life. I could still feel overwhelming love and moments of peace.

Every once in a while, the idea that everything I saw was an illusion and that I was actually alone in the universe since only I, Brahman, existed would give me a "freak-out moment." I would ignore those thoughts, push down those feelings, and create my own purpose.

I was now walking through life as two beings.

As the great yogis had done, I wished to kill off one of them...

And Then He Spoke

The Descending Ends

"What do you think? If a man has a hundred sheep,
and one of them has gone astray, does he not leave the
ninety-nine on the mountains and go in search of
the one that went astray?"

MATTHEW 18:12

"So now, I will break his yoke bar from upon you,
and I will tear off your shackles."

NAHUM 1:13 NIV

I LOOKED UP TO Yogananda a lot. I collected many of his books and tried to live and breathe yoga. The fact that Yogananda talked about "god" and Jesus so much caused me to finally crack open a Bible. I started reading some of the words of Jesus. It had been a long time since I had done that. I found Jesus to be very wise.

I signed up for a class about Jesus and the gospel of John through the Ananda website. Their goal was to show that Jesus taught Yogic concepts and that he was merely one of many "sons of god." As I took the class, I became aware of something... there was a lot of twisting of scripture going on. I wasn't even an actual Christian, and I could spot that. The points they were trying to make could not make sense if you looked at the Bible as a whole. They were taking many verses out of context. I felt like this was a red flag... "Maybe they just misunderstand the Bible?"

That situation reminds me of Bible verses like,

> *"Pay careful attention to yourselves and to all the flock, in which the Holy Spirit has made you overseers, to care for the church of God, which he obtained with his own blood. I know that after my departure fierce wolves will come in among you, not sparing the flock; and from among your own selves will arise men speaking twisted things, to draw away the disciples after them.."* (Acts 20:28-30), or *"For such men are false apostles, deceitful workmen, disguising themselves as apostles of Christ."* (2 Corinthians 11:13).

One day, I went outside for my morning meditation session. I got seated comfortably and started to breathe in and out deeply, just feeling the wind and sunshine. On a typical day, after settling in like this, I would start my process of seeing the world around me as a beautiful illusion and work on ego destruction. Today was different, though. I had a lot more on my mind. I pondered the reality of what "god" was and what I supposedly was. "Am I really the thing behind all that I see?"

I wondered what would happen if I opened the door one more time to ask if there was something more than all of this. I expected no answer that day, just the "universe" letting me know that "it" was all there was, in the way I learned from yoga. Something was pushing me to ask...

"To the creator God, whoever and whatever you might be, what is the truth?"

Immediately, I was surrounded by a powerful presence. It became very bright outside, so much so that the light seemed to blur my surroundings. As loud and beautiful as an orchestra, God imprinted into my soul, "I AM."

At that moment, I felt complete shock. I could hardly comprehend what had just happened. The God of the universe had just woken me up from a dream. I felt my senses come back to me, and a flood of truth poured into my head: "I am not god consciousness," "I am a separate being from the things around me," "Brahman is a false god," "Evil does exist," and so much more.

For those who don't know, The I AM is the God spoken of in the Bible. I knew who was talking to me, but I didn't know the details of what that could mean. I did not suddenly start believing that all of the Bible was true or that Jesus was the Son of God. All I knew was that the Bible writers had written about their experiences with this God.

I did know that God called me out of the non-reality I had been stuck in and wanted me to pursue Him. He left no room for me to doubt by being so clear and loud! I considered this a great act of mercy and compassion. He did not have to answer me or make His presence that clear and solid for me. To this day, I believe He did this to answer the prayers of my friends and family, who could see I lost my way. I gave Him that opening with my specific question, and He kicked down every door that stood between us at that moment. Prayer really works...

I was hungry for more truth, and I asked God to give me answers to all my questions. Here are some examples of the questions that were going through my head...

"How much of the Bible is meant to be taken literally?"

"Has any of the Bible been tampered with over time?"

"Was Jesus actually the Messiah, or should I only study the Old Testament to learn about God?"

"If God is all good, why does evil exist?"

I had many more questions than these and knew I needed to look into things immediately. By divine providence, I was already working at a Christian bookstore, so I had a lot of resources. God made it clear to me that He broke my chains that day. I was only going to accept very clear answers to my questions. I know how to poke holes in arguments, and I was ready to do that with any answers that didn't make sense.

I did lots of research on the accuracy of the Bible. I wanted to see what Christian and non-Christian historians had to say about it, as well as the arguments about what was to be taken literally and what wasn't. There was a lot of great information. Christians of various kinds may differ with some of their answers to these questions, but I learned what I needed to know to form my own opinion based on all of the facts we have.

God gifted me with many books I would need along the way. It was no coincidence that I would have a specific question, and then a book that answered that question would appear in the "free damaged books" area where I worked the very next day.

Sometimes, I would have a new question, and later, I would overhear a few of our customers discussing that topic in depth. I would always double-check the accuracy of the information I overheard. I loved being in an environment where discussions like these could take place.

Once, I had a customer come up to the cash register and buy a Bible concordance, which I happened to have wanted to better understand the Bible. After paying for it, he handed it to me. I was surprised and asked, "What is this for?" He told me he knew I was supposed to have it.

I became friends with many of my co-workers and had opportunities to ask them about their beliefs as Christians. There was one person in particular that I became very close with. Her name is Claudia, and her passion for God really stood out to me. She was kind and would invite me over for dinner and Bible discussions. I tended to make a person's head spin with all my deep questions, but she was very patient with me. If she didn't have an answer to something, we could try to find the answers together. She was very generous to me and even bought me some of the informational books she would see me eyeing up at the bookstore where we worked. I will always be grateful for our friendship.

Another great thing happened in my life after God came in. When I was younger, God spoke to me in my dreams. When I left Christianity, the dreams stopped. I was really excited that when I started hearing God's voice again, He began speaking to me in my dreams again!

My favorite books at our store were the ones from the Christian Apologetics section. Apologetics is a genre that tackles tough questions. It answers the question of why a person would believe anything in Christianity. It reviews historical and archeological proofs and logic-based arguments on questions like morality and the existence of God. I was surprised at how much information there is out there! Even many Christians don't realize how much evidence we have.

To my Christian friends, I implore you to look into the answers we have for life's hard questions and the evidence we have for what is in the Bible.

"But in your hearts honor Christ the Lord as holy, always being prepared to make a defense to anyone who asks you for a reason for the hope that is in you; yet do it with gentleness and respect." (1 Peter 3:15)

Yes, you may believe because of how God has personally worked in your life, and you have no reason to doubt Him. Still, some very skeptical people might need some concrete information to go along with hearing your experience. You never know who you can reach just by knowing more of the information we have available to us.

So, what about Jesus? Who was Jesus Christ? He is the Son of God. We have several eyewitness accounts that He was here, performed miracles, died on a cross, and resurrected from the dead. Those are some big claims. I was very skeptical about that whole situation. However, I learned about some excellent arguments that made me see this was no ordinary Jewish teacher.

First, many sources outside the Bible confirm Jesus was a real person and was absolutely here. This is some of what non-Christian historians have agreed on:

- Jesus was a teacher
- Both friend and foe of Jesus believed He was working miracles.
- Jesus was crucified in Jerusalem under Pontius Pilate
- The New Testament writers believed that Jesus had risen from the grave (Stewart)

There are also non-Christian resources from that time period that confirm other points about Jesus's life. Here are just a couple:

- Jesus was known to be wise and virtuous (Historian Josephus in *Antiquities of the Jews*)
- Celsus, a 2nd-century Greek philosopher and a fierce opponent of Christianity, confirmed Jesus was known as a miracle worker ("Contra Celsum")

After Jesus's death and resurrection, his disciples spread the news to everyone they could. Many of them were murdered or executed. Unless they really believed that they saw Jesus after he was resurrected, why would they put themselves through all of that? They weren't making money from it. They made many enemies doing it. People aren't so willing to die for what they know to be a lie.

Besides the many sources that give us information about Jesus and His teachings, we can also see the many lives that have changed because of Him now. We don't just have to read about Jesus; we can experience Him in our lives—millions of people today do!

Most world religions teach that one must try to reach heaven, moksha, oneness, paradise, nirvana, etc., through one's own works. Christianity is unique because it is the only religion where God reaches down to man.

If you haven't heard the gospel message, let me explain it to you. I like Ray Comfort's teaching method, so I will use it. I highly recommend checking out his YouTube videos. He is very inspirational.

So, first off, are you afraid of death? No? Being buried underground and the whole death process doesn't sound very appealing. Yes, it happens to us all, but something deep in you wants to live.

Next question: Do you believe in God? Yes? Cool, we will get to that. Did you answer no? Do you know what the default position is if you are an atheist? That means you believe the scientific impossibility that nothing created everything or that everything came out of nothing. That is a challenging position to defend, being impossible!

Look at a building. Is there any proof there was a builder? Buildings don't build themselves. The building is absolute proof there was a builder. A painting is absolute proof there was a painter. Creation is absolute proof there was a creator. Birds, the sky, the miracle of the human eye, childbirth, and so much more! All of these things show us God's creative hand.

So, do you think God could be the answer to death? If He made us, we should find out why we die. If you haven't read the Bible, I highly recommend it. There is a reason it is the top-selling book of all time in the entire world. In the Old Testament of the Bible, God promised to destroy death. The New Testament tells us how he did it.

What does the Bible say death is actually? It says it is wages. Isn't that interesting?

"For the wages of sin is death, but the free gift of God is eternal life in Christ Jesus our Lord." (Romans 6:23)

In other words, God is paying you in death for your sins. A judge is looking at a criminal who thinks lightly of killing three women. He says, "They were prostitutes, judge. They were the scum of society." The judge says, "I will show you how serious this is. I'm giving you the death sentence. This is what you've earned, your wages, what we are paying you."

We don't take sin very seriously, but the Bible says that sin is serious to a holy God. Your death is evidence that your sin is serious to Him. Do you think that God is justified in giving you the death sentence? Are you that evil that He is justified in doing that? Or do you think you are a good person? Most people will answer yes and say that, in general, they are morally good. Let's test that out. We will use the Bible's Ten Commandments as a moral measuring rod.

How many lies have you told? What do you call someone who has told lies? A liar. Even if it was small, have you ever stolen something before? That makes you a thief. Have you ever used God's name in vain? Do you love your mom? Would you ever use her name as a swear word? If you would, that is breaking the commandment about honoring your father and mother. If you wouldn't, then why would you use the name of the God who gave you your mom in such a way? That's called blasphemy, and it is a very serious thing. Punishable by death in the Old Testament.

Hang in there. We are almost done with these questions. Jesus said that if you have ever even looked with lust at someone, you have committed adultery in your heart. Have you ever done that? So here is the judgment: if you have said yes to all of these things, you are a lying, thieving, blaspheming adulterer at heart. So, you have earned your wages.

When God judges you based on the Ten Commandments, which is the moral law, will you be found innocent or guilty? We would all be found guilty. Heaven or hell? Hell. That should concern you. So, what did God do for guilty sinners so they wouldn't have to be condemned in this way? Have you heard about Jesus dying on the cross? Most people have, but you may not understand what that means. If you can understand this next point, it could change everything.

You and I broke the moral law, but Jesus paid the fine. If you are in court for a speeding ticket but someone else pays the price for you, the judge can legally let you go. God can legally dismiss your case and take the death sentence off of you, all because of Jesus's death and resurrection. All you have to do is repent of your sins, which means to turn from them and trust in Jesus. Everlasting life is a free gift from the Savior.

I hope you will think about all of this. When are you going to repent and accept Jesus's gift? I hope it will be today. Why not now?

The End of Yoga in My Life

So, what about Yoga? It hadn't just been my spiritual path; it had also been my career path. Could I still teach this practice?

One day, while I was at work, a missionary came in and asked if we had a copy of *Death of a Guru*. He explained what it was about, and it caught my attention. I ordered it shortly after that conversation. The author of that book came from a more traditional Hindu background. It revealed a lot about the caste system and how Hindus of those paths taught things.

That's when it hit me that maybe I had been fed a version of Hinduism that could cater to a Western audience. This was not the yogic Hinduism I had come to know from Yogananda. I didn't really feel good about this religion anymore. I found that I had just kind of quit meditating, doing yoga, and other Hindu practices. I was too busy reading the Bible, praying, and reading books on theology and apologetics.

At this point, my question was, can I really continue calling the exercises I was teaching people yoga? Would I even want to? My grandmother had given me her friend's email a while back. Maybe it was finally time to contact him.

Ivan Raj, who grew up in India and attended a Hindu school, has been trying to teach Christians the truth about yoga. He is the founder of *Yoga Unboxed*, which I highly recommend everyone, Christian or otherwise, check out. He has tons of great information. I emailed Ivan my arguments and background to see what he would say. What he revealed to me about these practices in his email back was very eye-opening...

Firstly, popular sequences like Sun Salutations (Surya Namaskara) really are things Hindus use to worship Shiva. Some try to Christianize yoga and say they can worship the Son of God doing it instead of the sun god. The Bible says in Deuteronomy 12:4 (NLT)

> *"Do not worship the LORD your God in the way these pagan peoples worship their gods."*

Many verses ask us not to mimic what the pagans do, so even if we weren't using it for worship, we aren't supposed to be taking part in things pagan religions have created.

The second red flag pointed out to me was that the chants and songs we would sing in school were not just peace chants. They were songs actually used to worship Hindu deities. I read some of the translations in English and saw that in some of the songs, you were asking the gods to become one with you.

Perhaps it is no wonder then that many of the Christians I went to school with don't practice Christianity anymore. They still worship Jesus, but a lot of them don't believe He is the only Son of God anymore. They call themselves Christian, but they practice many things we are warned as Christians not to do. Don't get me wrong, they are lovely, intelligent people, but like me, they were slowly introduced to Hindu thought and started believing a lot of it.

The third red flag was when Ivan told me who was in charge of the Yoga Alliance, the organization that certified me and controlled my continuing education. I had a silly idea that these were just some hippy-type Americans who loved yoga. No, it turned out I had been certified by Hindu Swamis! These bits of information are only touching the surface...

I needed time to process all of this information. In the meantime, I picked up a book titled "*The Kingdom of the Cults Handbook*" from my bookstore. I was looking through the book's contents page when a title caught my attention: "New Age Spirituality—The Age of Aquarius." I discovered why I transitioned so easily from New Age to Hindu practices. Here is a quote from the book...

> *"In the late '60s and early '70s, Yogi Bhajan – who brought Kundalini Yoga to the West – began speaking about the Age of Aquarius, and said that the transition to the new era would begin in November 1991 and end on November 11, 2011. Then humankind would remain in the Aquarian Age for roughly 2,000 years."*[1]

I continued reading and realized that much of the New Age movement was heavily influenced by Yogic Hindu thought! Yoga has snuck into American culture through several different paths. In the '60s and '70s, many Hindu missionaries came to the U.S. wearing crosses and speaking about Jesus and yoga.

Ultimately, I realized I couldn't be a Christian and teach yoga. The Bible makes it very clear we are not supposed to use pagan-created practices. Plus, yoga is not exercise and stretching. It is a branch of Hinduism meant to yoke you to Brahman that happens to involve forms of stretching.

Yoga does not get to own any exercises or stretches, but it comprises sequences that must maintain a specific flow. This flow is supposed to produce a type of "inner alchemy" involving chakras and getting your mind into a certain state. It is also made up of Hindu worship sequences that cannot be Christianized, and many times tell stories of these Hindu gods. Also, to stay certified, you must continue to meet the requirements of the Hindu Swamis.

If you are a Christian teaching or practicing yoga, I encourage you to listen to the many stories of other people who came to God and, because of this, leave their teaching practices. I also encourage you to check out *Yoga Unboxed*. I am 100% sure you will learn things you have never been taught before that will change your perspective.

If you are not a Christian, and maybe rolling your eyes right now at the above statements, I would like to invite you if you haven't already accepted God into your life. Don't worry about the details right now; instead, I invite you to do what I did the day God made Himself known to me. Praying to "whoever" it was that created everything, to reveal the truth to you, whatever that could be. It couldn't hurt to try, right? What do you have to lose? Just be open to accepting truth no matter what the truth is, not closing the door to something just because you don't like it. I was on a journey for the truth, whether it was something I wanted to hear or not.

My story is a rescue story. I did nothing to deserve my rescue. Thank you to everyone who prayed for my rescue. I was finally baptized just two days before my birthday. I am so glad that I have God in my life. There is no spiritual path out there as fulfilling as being a follower of Christ.

For my final chapter, I would like to share some of the many things I have learned in Christian apologetics. I will focus on the archeological evidence.. I cannot list everything I have learned, as you could fill many books with a list that long, but I will point out a few things that jumped out to me personally. I will also provide resources for you to further your study of this topic.

Thank you so much for taking the time to read my story. I pray that God speaks to each and every one of your hearts...

Evidence to Consider

"When we come to the Bible and try to listen to its claims, we can easily misjudge those claims if we hear them only from within the framework of our own modern assumptions. Letting the Bible speak for itself, that is, letting it speak in its own terms, includes letting the Bible speak from within its own worldview rather than merely our own."[1]

VERN POYTHRESS

"It is not enough for the skeptic, then, to simply dismiss the Christian teaching about the resurrection of Jesus by saying, "It just couldn't have happened." He or she must face and answer all these historical questions: Why did Christianity emerge so rapidly, with such power? No other band of messianic followers in that era concluded their leader was raised from the dead—why did this group do so? No group of Jews ever worshipped a human being as God. What led them to do it? Jews did not believe in divine men or individual resurrections. What changed their worldview virtually overnight? How do you account for the hundreds of eyewitnesses to the resurrection who lived on for decades and publicly maintained their testimony, eventually giving their lives for their belief?"[2]

TIMOTHY KELLER, *THE REASON FOR GOD: BELIEF IN AN AGE OF SKEPTICISM*

What I am about to present to you here is merely a fraction of the huge amount of evidence we have that support the Bible's claims. Let's get started!

Historical Finds

- **Sumerian King List**: The Sumerians created one of the first civilizations in the ancient world. The list of kings that has been discovered was found in the ruins of Mesopotamia carved into clay tablets. Surviving copies of this list date back to around 2100 BCE. These lists named the kings who ruled and how long they ruled. In the middle of the list there is an interruption. It says, *"After the flood had swept over the earth and when kingship was lowered again from heaven..."* After this, the list of kings who ruled continues. The list is split between kings who ruled before the flood and those who ruled after it. Unless it was an actual event that had a major impact on humanity, why would this event be mentioned in a list of kings? Another thing to note is that *the kings who ruled before the flood seemed to have very unusually long lifespans*, just like the Bible says people did. The kings who are listed after the great flood did not live as long as their predecessors.
- **Flood Stories**: We find many flood stories from all around the world, in many different cultures. Many people have heard of *The Epic of Gilgamesh*. It is a story following the adventures of an ancient Babylonian king named Gilgamesh. The best copy of this tale was found in Ninevah, written on clay tablets. A hero from old that Gilgamesh speaks to tells him that a long time ago one of the gods warned him about a worldwide flood that was coming. He is told to build a ship and carry every kind of animal on it. He also uses a dove and raven to see if the waters had receded yet, just like in the Bible.

- **Hittite Capital**: About 100 years ago, critics said that the Hittite people constantly brought up in the Bible never actually existed. Since then, we have discovered the Hittite's capital city, Boghazkoy, in Turkey. As you are about to see, there are a lot of instances in which people claim something in the Bible is false, just to have something years later pop up, proving that it was true.
- **Haran**: Haran, modern day Harran in Turkey, bears the name of the father of Lot, brother of Abraham. (Genesis 11:27). Villages nearby bear the names of Abraham's great-grandfather and grandfather, Serug and Nahor. This all points to Abraham and his family actually existing.
- **City of Dan**: In modern day Laish (Dan) Israel, excavations show that a Canaanite city was destroyed and then rebuilt. The artifacts found there show that Israelites had then inhabited the rebuilt city. In the book of Judges, in the Bible, the children of Dan destroy a Canaanite city with fire and by sword. Afterwards, they build their own city right there and name it Dan.
- **Pharaoh Shishak's Record**: In 1 Kings 14 and 2 Chronicles 12, the Egyptian Pharaoh Shishak is recorded to have invaded Judah during the reign of Rehoboam. In Egypt, in the Karnak Temple of Amun, a record of this event had been found carved into the wall. The Shishak Relief was made to commemorate Shishak's victory over Rehoboam when he robbed Solomon's temple of treasures.
- **Tel Dan Inscription**: The Tel Dan inscription found inscribed in stone was a very important find in 1993 and 1994. It was the first reference found to King David that wasn't in the Bible. It says "The house of David" along with mention of a "king of Israel." This find wasn't all that long ago and I think it is important to state that *the more time goes by, the more evidence we find for what is written in the Bible.*

- **The House of Yahweh**: Dated between 835 and 796 BCE, this ostracon appears to be something like a receipt. It was a donation to the House of Yahweh (Solomon's temple) of 3 shekels of silver.
- **Royal Court Seals**: These seals that were found were used to press into clay which sealed up documents of the king. These ones date between 900 and 600 BCE. Seals were found for Hezekiah, Uzziah, and Hoshea. There was also one that said, "belonging to Shema, servant of Jeroboam."
- **Mesha Stele**: This stone has inscribed on it the accomplishments of Mesha, king of Moab. The stone mentions that King Omri and his son Ahab humbled Moab but that after Ahab's death, King Mesha triumphed over Israel. 2 Kings 3 tells part of this story as well in the Bible.
- **Obelisk of Shalmaneser**: The Assyrian King Shalmaneser III was an enemy of Israel. On this obelisk you can see the conquests of the king. One part of it shows Jehu, king of Israel, kneeling and offering tribute to the king. 2 Kings 9-10 mentions the reign of King Jehu.
- **Siloam Tunnel Inscription**: This inscription celebrates this tunnel's completion, which was ordered to be made in the days of King Hezekiah. It was carved into the stone wall of the tunnel. The tunnel is mentioned in both 2 Kings 20:20 and 2 Chronicles 32:30.
- **The Tomb of the Hezir Family**: Located in the Kidron Valley of Jerusalem there is an inscription identifying a burial cave as belonging to the descendants of Hezir. The names of 3 generations of this family also appear. This verifies this priestly family that was mentioned in 1 Chronicles 24:15 and Nehemiah 10:20.
- **The Pontius Pilate Inscription**: Dating back to the time of Jesus, in the ruins of Caesarea Maritima, there is a stone bearing Pontius Pilate's name. This is important because until the 1960's, the only place you could find his name was

- **The Tomb of Caiaphas**: Caiaphas was the priest that brought Jesus to trail. Discovered in 1990 was a burial cave near Jerusalem with the bones of a family. One of the names on a stone box of bones was Caiaphas. It is believed that this was the Caiaphas family tomb.
- **Pool of Siloam**: According to John 9, the Pool of Siloam was where Jesus healed a blind man. For a long time, scholars argued that the Pool of Siloam didn't exist in Jesus's time. The pool was discovered in 2005. This is another example of the truth being revealed over time.

(All above information can be found in more detail in "Rose Book of Bible Charts, Maps & Time Lines" 48-59)

Besides these bits of information, there are also many Greco-Roman references to Jesus. They confirm the facts that he existed, was Jewish, had a following, and was crucified on a cross. There is so much information out there! People have filled books with all the evidences we have for what the Bible claims. What I listed above was just a small taste of it.

The Bible also has many famously fulfilled prophecies. There are far too many of them to go over in this book in detail, but I will list a few of them here. I encourage you to do some of your own research into the miracle of fulfilled prophecies of the Bible.

- One hundred fifty years before Cyrus the Great came to the throne, the prophet Isaiah wrote this about him:

"Thus says the Lord to his anointed, to Cyrus, whom he has taken by his right hand to subdue nations before him and strip the loins of kings, to force gateways before him that their gates be closed no more: I will go before you levelling the heights. I will shatter the bronze gateways, smash the iron bars. I will give you the hidden

treasures, the secret hoards, that you may know that I am the Lord." (Isaiah 45:1-3)

- Daniel has a vision of a ram (Medo-Persia) with uneven horns attacking all the animals in his way. It couldn't be stopped until a goat (Greece) with a giant horn (Alexander the Great) shattered the ram's horns and trampled the ram until he died. When he conquers the ram, his own horn breaks off, and four horns grow from his head (Alexander's generals). One of these horns grows a boastful horn who makes war against the Jews (Antiochus Epiphanes). There is a lot more that he predicts but this is just a sample of it.

"And he said, "Look, I am making known to you what shall happen in the latter time of the indignation; for at the appointed time the end shall be. The ram which you saw, having the two horns—they are the kings of Media and Persia. And the male goat is the kingdom of Greece. The large horn that is between its eyes is the first king. As for the broken horn and the four that stood up in its place, four kingdoms shall arise out of that nation, but not with its power." (Daniel 8:19-22)

- Jesus fulfilled many prophecies. The messiah was to be born in Bethlehem (Micah 2:5), he would be born of a virgin (Isaiah 7:14), and he would be sold for thirty pieces of silver (Zechariah 11:13). These are just a few examples, but Jesus actually fulfilled many more prophecies from the Old Testament.

While I cannot go over everything in this book, I hope I have given you something to think about. I would like to end with a list of resources I have found incredibly helpful to me on my journey. If you would like more information on prophecy, evidence, or intellectual

Evidence to Consider

and moral arguments, I highly recommend these resources. I have also listed some sources of others who had journeys that lead them to God. May the Holy Spirit lead you as you explore!

Books

- *The Story of Reality* by Gregory Koukl
- *If God is Good* by Randy Alcorn
- *Is God a Moral Monster?* by Paul Copan
- *The Reason for God* by Timothy Keller
- *I Don't Have Enough Faith to Be an Atheist* by Norman Geisler and Frank Turek
- *Seeking Allah, Finding Jesus* by Nabeel Qureshi
- *Death of a Guru* by Rabi Maharaj
- *The Unknown God* by Mathew John
- *Why Believe the Bible* by John MacArthur
- *How We Got the Bible* by Timothy Paul Jones, PhD
- *Evidence for Jesus* by Josh and Sean McDowell
- *Eternity in Their Hearts* by Don Richardson
- *Evidence that Demands a Verdict* by Josh and Sean McDowell

YouTube Channels

- Sean McDowell
- Cross Examined
- Capturing Christianity
- Mike Winger
- Delafé Testimonies

Encouragement From the Bible

"So do not fear, for I am with you; do not be dismayed, for I am your God. I will strengthen you and help you; I will uphold you with my righteous right hand." - Isaiah 41:10 (NIV)

"I sought the LORD, and He answered me and delivered me from all my fears. Those who look to Him are radiant, and their faces shall never be ashamed. Oh, taste and see that the LORD is good! Blessed is the man who takes refuge in Him!" - Psalm 34: 4-5, 8 (ESV)

"In the world you will have tribulation. But take heart; I have overcome the world."- John 16:33 (ESV)

"Come to me, all who labor and are heavy laden, and I will give you rest." - Matthew 11:28 (ESV)

"Peace I leave with you; my peace I give to you. Not as the world gives do I give to you. Let not your hearts be troubled, neither let them be afraid." - John 14:27 (ESV)

"They shall hunger no more, neither thirst anymore; the sun shall not strike them, nor any scorching heat. For the Lamb in the midst of the throne will be their shepherd, and he will guide them to springs of living water, and God will wipe away every tear from their eyes." Revelation 7:16-17 (ESV)

Notes

Chapter 1: God Created Man... Or Maybe Man Created God

1. Richard Dawkins' Speech at the Edinburgh International Science Festival (April 15, 1992); quoted in "EDITORIAL: A scientist's case against God," "The Independent"(London), (p. 17), April 20, 1992

Chapter 2: Stay Wild, Moon Child

1. Silver RavenWolf (2011). "Solitary Witch: The Ultimate Book of Shadows for the New Generation," p.23, Llewellyn Worldwide
2. Bowling, Suzanna. "A Journey of Healing: Masaru Emoto." T2conline.com, 2 Dec. 2022, t2conline.com/a-journey-of-healing-masaru-emoto/.
3. Joy, Rebecca. "How Does a Full Moon Affect Our Physical and Mental Well-Being?" Healthline.com, 26 Aug. 2022, www.healthline.com/health/full-moon-effects#about.
4. Lamb, Rachel. "Fact or Fiction: Does a Full Moon Affect Hospitals?" Yourworldhealthcare.com, 3 May 2019, www.yourworldhealthcare.com/uk/news/fact-or-fiction-does-a-full-moon-affect-hospitals.
5. "Riitta Klint." Goodreads.com, www.goodreads.com/quotes/9249230-stay-wild-moon-child-i-will-shine-my-full-silver#:~:text=I%20will%20shine%20my%20full%20silver%20light%20on%20your%20path,yourself%20stay%20wild%20and%20true.

Chapter 3: It's Just Exercise, Right?

1. "130 Inspiring Quotes by Sadhguru." Yogi.Press, 27 Apr. 2020, www.yogi.press/home/inspiring-quotes-by-sadhguru#:~:text=%E2%80%9CYoga%20is%20not%20just%20exercise,your%20own%20nature.%E2%80%9D%20%E2%80%94%20Sadhguru.
2. Western Yoga College Teacher Training Manual. Scott Miller, 2018.
3. "Kundalini Yoga." Wikipedia, Wikimedia Foundation, 14 Nov. 2023, en.wikipedia.org/wiki/Kundalini_yoga.
4. "What Is Kundalini Meditation." Verywellmind.com, 27 Nov. 2022, www.verywellmind.com/what-is-kundalini-meditation-4688618.

Chapter 4: That Which You Think, You Attract

1. "Esther Hicks." AZQuotes.com. Wind and Fly LTD, 2024. 17 March 2024. https://www.azquotes.com/quote/561134
2. "7 Habits that made me a Millionaire in 2 years" *YouTube*, uploaded by Aaron Doughty 27 August 2021 https://www.youtube.com/watch?v=yQdcHQTXwGM&t=1s&ab_channel=AaronDoughty
3. "About Abraham-Hicks." Abraham-hicks.Com, (n.d) www.abraham-hicks.com/about/.
4. "The Truth About the Law of Attraction." Psychology Today, 18 Sept. 2016, www.psychologytoday.com/us/blog/the-blame-game/201609/the-truth-about-the-law-attraction#:~:text=Key%20points,achieved%2C%20no%20matter%20how%20unrealistic.

Chapter 5: Tat Tvam Asi – That Thou Art

1. "Vivekachudamani of Adi Shankaracharya." VivikaVani, 19 May 2018, vivekavani.com/vc/.
2. Sarvapriyananda, Swami "Who am I if not the knower" *YouTube*, uploaded by Vedanta Society 07 October 2023

Notes

Chapter 6: The Death of Self
1. "Rajneesh." AZQuotes.com. Wind and Fly LTD, 2024. 17 March 2024. https://www.azquotes.com/quote/545909
2. "Depersonalization-Derealization Disorder." Cleveland Clinic, 29 Sept. 2023, my.clevelandclinic.org/health/diseases/9791-depersonalization-derealization-disorder.

Chapter 7: And Then He Spoke
1. Kingdom of the Cults Handbook. Bethany House Publishers, 2020.

Chapter 8: Evidence to Consider
1. "Quotes on the Truthfulness and Reliability of the Bible." The Gospel Coalition, 23 Nov. 2013, www.thegospelcoalition.org/blogs/trevin-wax/quotes-on-the-truthfulness-and-reliability-of-the-bible/.
2. "Timothy J. Keller Quotes." Goodreads, (n.d), www.goodreads.com/quotes/1120879-it-is-not-enough-for-the-skeptic-then-to-simply.

Made in the USA
Columbia, SC
20 October 2024